**Donated
To The Library by**

YELLOWSTONE

FIRST of the LAST
WILD PLACES

BY

GEORGE B. ROBINSON

SIERRA PRESS
MARIPOSA, CA

DEDICATION:

To Kae, my wife, my best friend, the keeper of my heart, and the source of my abiding sense of wonder. She reads everything that I write and it is better because of her. Sadly, she knows too well that writing is a thief of time. —G.B.R.

ACKNOWLEDGMENTS:

My enduring thanks to my father who introduced me to the National Parks when I was two years old. He started me on a long journey to Yellowstone. I am also grateful to my former colleagues at Yellowstone for sharing with me their knowledge of "Wonderland." They know who they are. Finally, I will always think of Jeff Nicholas at Sierra Press, and my editor Nicky Leach as more than publishing professionals. They are good friends, who share my passion for words and writing. —G.B.R.

FRONT COVER:
Old Faithful erupting. PHOTO © JEFF VANUGA.
INSIDE FRONT COVER:
Bull elk and harem in mist, early morning .
PHOTO © DIANA STRATTON.
TITLE PAGE:
Bison herd and steam from Midway Geyser Basin.
PHOTO © DIANA STRATTON.
THIS PAGE (RIGHT):
Lower Falls of the Yellowstone River, Grand Canyon of the Yellowstone.
PHOTO © GLENN VAN NIMWEGEN.
THIS PAGE (BELOW):
Gray wolf pup. PHOTO © TOM & PAT LEESON.
PAGE 6/7:
Bison grazing in Hayden Valley, early morning.
PHOTO © JON GNASS.
PAGE 7 (BOTTOM RIGHT):
Bubbling mudpot in Pocket Basin.
PHOTO © JEFF GNASS

4

CONTENTS

THE SETTING:

Petrified log with currant bush on Specimen Ridge.   PHOTO © SCOTT T. SMITH

*Places circle in my mind like gifting birds…Small, quick
perceptions the gifting birds leave me…Some I can put together,
not as a story or theory, but a sense of life, of place…Random
perceptions become groups of experiences, pieces tumbling
in…Puzzle pieces without jigsaw cuts to define them.*
                              —Charles Jones, *The Gifting Birds*

Yellowstone is both a real place, and a state of mind. It is a powerful elixir for me—the kind place of where author Barry Lopez has suggested that I can renegotiate my contracts with Nature. Because I have worked in national parks my entire life, I feel a special kinship with Yellowstone, and I am grateful for its gifts to me.

In a way, Yellowstone is both beginning and end of a long personal odyssey. My journey to Yellowstone began 60 years ago, when my father accepted a job in Lassen Volcanic National Park in northern California. Those early years foretold a time when I, too, would work in a geological wonderland.

As a child I was enchanted by the idea of Yellowstone's wonders. I thumbed through photographs of Old Faithful, Yellowstone Falls, and grizzly bears in books and magazines, and my teacher talked about the park in school. I formed a mental picture of what it must be like. In Lassen, I saw fumaroles and hot springs. I watched steam venting from the cool summit of Lassen Peak. My father told me how ancient Mount Tehama had collapsed inward to form a huge crater called a caldera. I often saw bears and other large animals. Surely, I thought, Yellowstone must be like these things.

I visited Yellowstone with my father when I was a youngster, but I only remember seeing some of its popular icons—Old Faithful, Yellowstone Lake, Mammoth Hot Springs, some bears. Like many folks, my visit was cursory and superficial. I did not return to Yellowstone until the last few years of my career as a Chief of Interpretation, and it was only then that I began to see that there was much more to this wonderland than the things that I had dreamed about and seen in my youth. Of course, there were hundreds of facts and figures to learn—many of which I soon

forgot—but each day in Yellowstone, "gifting birds" brought new and precious fragments of thought and feeling that began to merge into a deeper understanding of meaning and place.

I am not a photographer, yet everywhere in Yellowstone my eyes take hundreds of pictures, all perfectly focused, composed, and exposed. I keep those images in my mind's album, where I can recall them whenever I long to return to Yellowstone. Opening the album I find a hillside carpeted with spring wildflowers exploding with colors like a van Gogh painting. On another page I see an infant stream rising in an alpine meadow more than two miles above the sea that will inevitably claim it. As the pages turn, other images unfold. I see fluted colonnades of ancient volcanic rock, a trout struggling upstream to spawn, a marmot sunning itself on a talus slope. On still another page I see an iridescent dragonfly wing, a fawn standing for the first time on wobbly legs, a waterfall concealed by a winter shroud of ice. Thumbing through my mental images I can watch Old Faithful erupt again, recall the spectacle of the great fires of 1988, and see a dipper walk under water in search of food.

Each time I open the album I am enchanted once more by Yellowstone, but I am reminded too that only as a manifestation of an idea, a dream realized, have people shaped this place. No human thought or actions have sculpted its features, or filled its ecological niches with abundant and diverse life forms. Again I sense that there is a rhythm to nature—a subtle flow of energy that Eastern philosophers call *chi*—that links all things. In Yellowstone, wild things move to a different cadence than we do. It is slow, measured, and harmonious.

Practitioners of the ancient Chinese art of *feng shui* believe that the spirit or atmosphere of a place influences our physical and emotional well-being. *Feng shui* masters are sensitive to the essence of things, and they manipulate, combine, and blend the parts of living and working spaces to enhance their influence on people. In Yellowstone, natural process is like a *feng shui* master, arranging all of the elements in the house of nature in the most harmonious way. In these mountains, nature has woven a complex fabric of shapes,

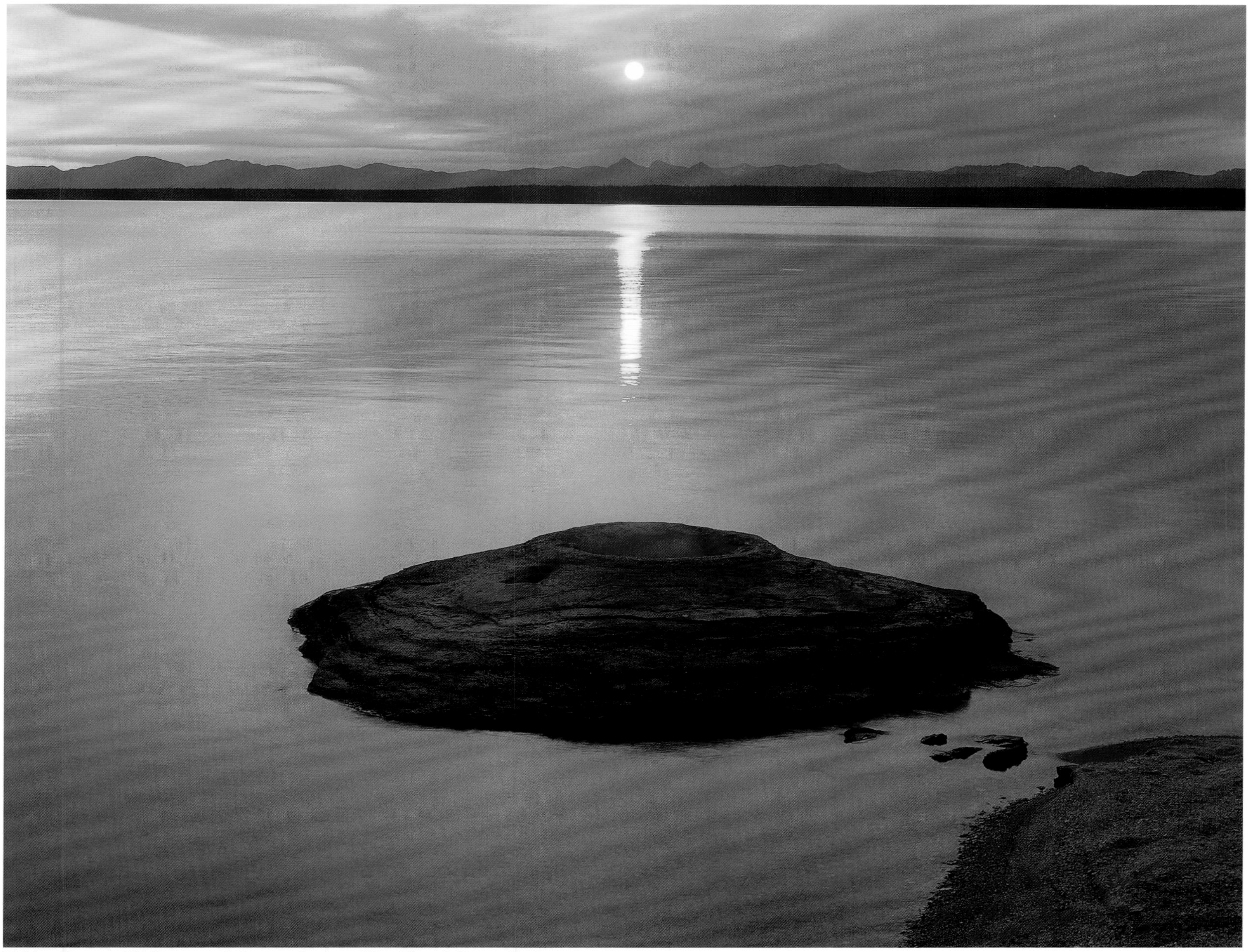

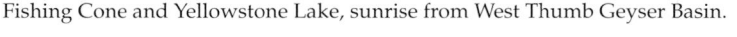

Fishing Cone and Yellowstone Lake, sunrise from West Thumb Geyser Basin.

hard and soft, large and small; a network of lines crossing lines; angles folded upon angles; circles within circles; a full spectrum of colors; the basic pattern of natural order that Zen philosophers refer to as *li*.

I have a covenant with Yellowstone. To fully experience it, I must come to understand and appreciate it, to see the pattern, to comprehend the meaning of its *li*. When I allow the place to envelop me, I can feel its rhythm, the flow of its *chi*. I can see the beautiful complexity of its *li* revealed. I can sense its palpable wild spirit. I can listen to its countless stories told in opposites of light and shadow, birth and death, winter and summer. I can have a perfect moment in a perfect place.

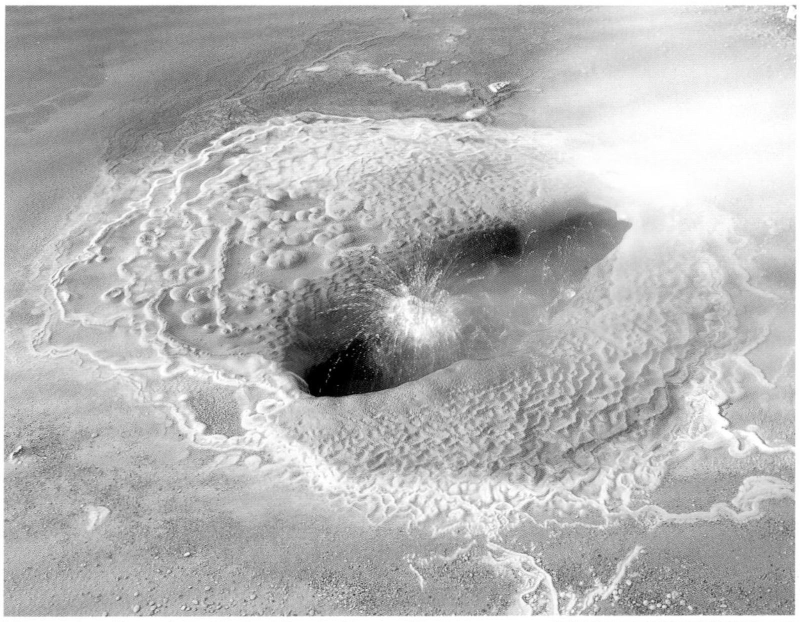

Hot spring, Porcelain Basin, Norris Geyser Basin.

An intricate web of interaction connects all life into one vast, self-maintaining system. Each part is related to every other part and we are all part of the whole…
—Lyall Watson, *Supernature*

Animals, plants, and the ecological processes that bind them together neither see, nor respect, the boundaries that people have drawn. Acknowledging these ecological truths, scientists and resource managers have increasingly looked beyond the park's legal boundaries for relationships and connections. With the park as a central element, they have defined a Greater Yellowstone Ecosystem—a description that aptly conveys a sense of both the remarkable size and the great significance of the area. Unfortunately, large ecosystems can become disarticulated patchworks of differing uses under federal, state, city, and private jurisdiction.

The Greater Yellowstone Ecosystem is an aggregation of countless smaller systems. Each is discrete and essentially self-sustaining, yet all are connected through the intricate and precisely ordered mechanisms of ecological process that extend beyond the park—like a great vascular system, resource managers know that they must care for the vessels as well as the heart. The greater ecosystem represents the whole organism, not just one of its organs. It is an affirmation that, ecologically, the whole is greater than the sum of its parts. It is the larger context of life and environment in which each smaller system operates, and upon which they rely for their health and vitality.

Activities beyond the boundary of Yellowstone can profoundly and irrevocably affect the resources within. For example, efforts to tap geothermal energy sources on private lands outside the park could seriously, and irreversibly, alter the conditions that give rise to Yellowstone's unique geothermal features because the underground watercourse is shared. Bison that wander beyond the park boundary are culled because they are believed to threaten domestic livestock with Brucellosis, but excessive control could seriously diminish the resident bison population. Toxic chemicals from upstream mine tailings could contaminate streams, lakes, and groundwater supplies dramatically altering riparian

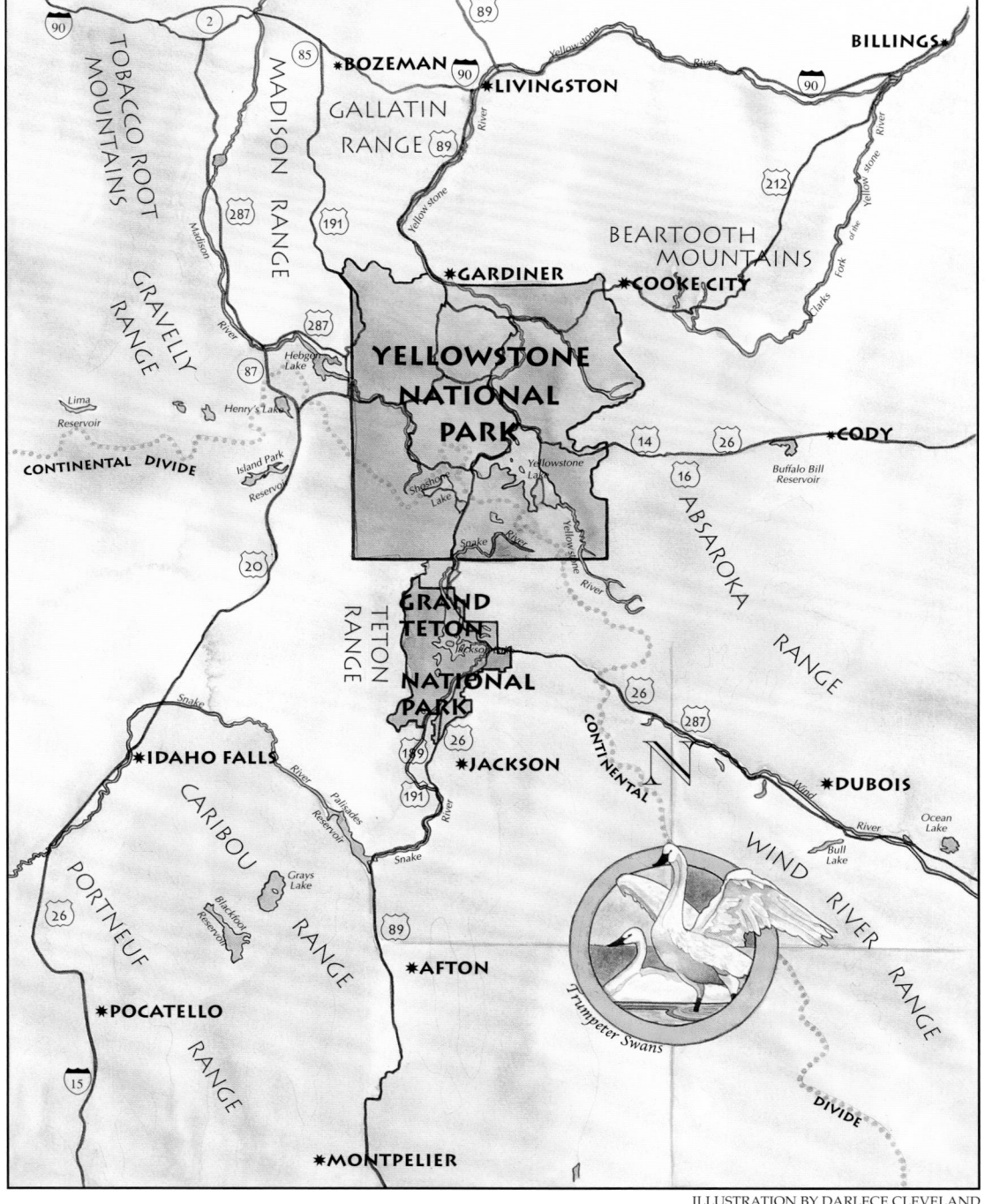

ILLUSTRATION BY DARLECE CLEVELAND

habitats and one of the most significant trout fisheries in North America. Logging, oil and gas exploration, and recreational development could further fragment the habitats of grizzly bears and wild ungulates.

Yellowstone National Park is just the 3,472 square-mile core of a larger system covering about 28,000 square miles. Most of the park is in Wyoming, but small parts of it lie in Montana and Idaho. The Greater Yellowstone Ecosystem includes Grand Teton National Park, seven national forests, three national wildlife refuges, and a variety of lands managed by the Bureau of Land Management.

PAGE 12 & 13: Firehole River flowing toward Midway Geyser Basin. PHOTO © LAURENCE PARENT

THE PARK:

Grizzly bear roams snow-covered Hayden Valley.   PHOTO © DIANA STRATTON

The air is cool, the azure sky cloudless. I have taken a few moments to enjoy the view before joining others at the summit of Mount Washburn. From my resting place on a lichen-encrusted rock I overlook the vast central plateau—all that remains of the immense caldera that formed when Yellowstone's heart burst 600,000 years ago. A few yards away, beyond some whitebark pine trees, the south face of Mount Washburn drops off abruptly, as if peeled away by a giant chisel. The precipice marks the place where part of the mountain dropped into the crater. Far away to the south, the Tetons jut into a limpid sky that brings them into sharp detail.

I am so intently focused on the grand vista that I barely notice something closer at hand. At first, I hear it. A muffled thump like a heavy footstep. Then another. And another. I quickly check to see if an animal is stalking me. Relieved that no hungry carnivore is in sight, I turn my attention again to the noise. This time I see a cone of a whitebark pine falling, taking its place among several others. Suddenly, a frenetic red squirrel appears among the cones. Having temporarily abandoned his harvest, the energetic bundle of reddish-brown fur grasps one of the cones and bounds off to store it in a secret midden. Later, perhaps just after she stirs from a long winter sleep, a grizzly bear hungry for pine nuts will find it in a cache long forgotten by the squirrel.

This miniature drama cannot rival the spectacle of the volcanic landscape, yet it reminds me that there are small things here too, and that they play a big part in the life and times of Yellowstone. To truly know this place, I must celebrate the small—take pleasure in the sparrow as well as the eagle, be a champion of the ordinary and inconspicuous.

My curiosity sated, I return to my musing. When I think about the essence of Yellowstone—as I often do—I am reminded of the paintings of artists Bev Doolittle and Charles Harper whose intent is to open the eyes of viewers, to cultivate in them the facility to look beyond the obvious.

These painters' interpretations of wild places and things often include barely discernible images of wildlife imbedded in the rocks, water, sky, and vegetation—subtle suggestions of the inseparable connections among all wild things and the nurturing earth. An indication that no creature, and no natural process, stands alone.

When I examine one of those paintings with a discerning eye, I make many unexpected discoveries. A dominant theme is obvious; yet, in some of them, I have found dozens of concealed animals, large and small. Each time I look at the painting I see something new, and always, every stone, every branch, every leaf and pine cone, every eye, paw, hoof, feather, and antler is fully and perfectly formed in its natural colors.

Thus it is in the painting called Yellowstone. Nature has added to her canvas obvious and spectacular touches: a giant crater, geysers, hot springs, and boiling mudpots; bear, moose, elk, bison; canyons, lakes, and waterfalls. But the canvas is replete too with many ordinary things, because in the economy of nature all things have value. Here I see the truth that all creatures, from the largest and most obvious, to the smallest, inconspicuous organisms, fill special niches and play important roles in an unending ecological drama. One organism depends on another. One community merges with the next. One process is inextricably linked with all others. Yellowstone's signature themes are composites of myriad smaller ones. I lived in Yellowstone National Park for 10 years, but each time I return to it I serendipitously find something new. Each visit offers an epiphany—a sudden, unexpected revelation of truth and meaning.

There is no shortage of spectacle in Yellowstone. The features—and the facts and figures about them—are impressive: the largest, the tallest, the deepest, the first, the last. They are emblematic of

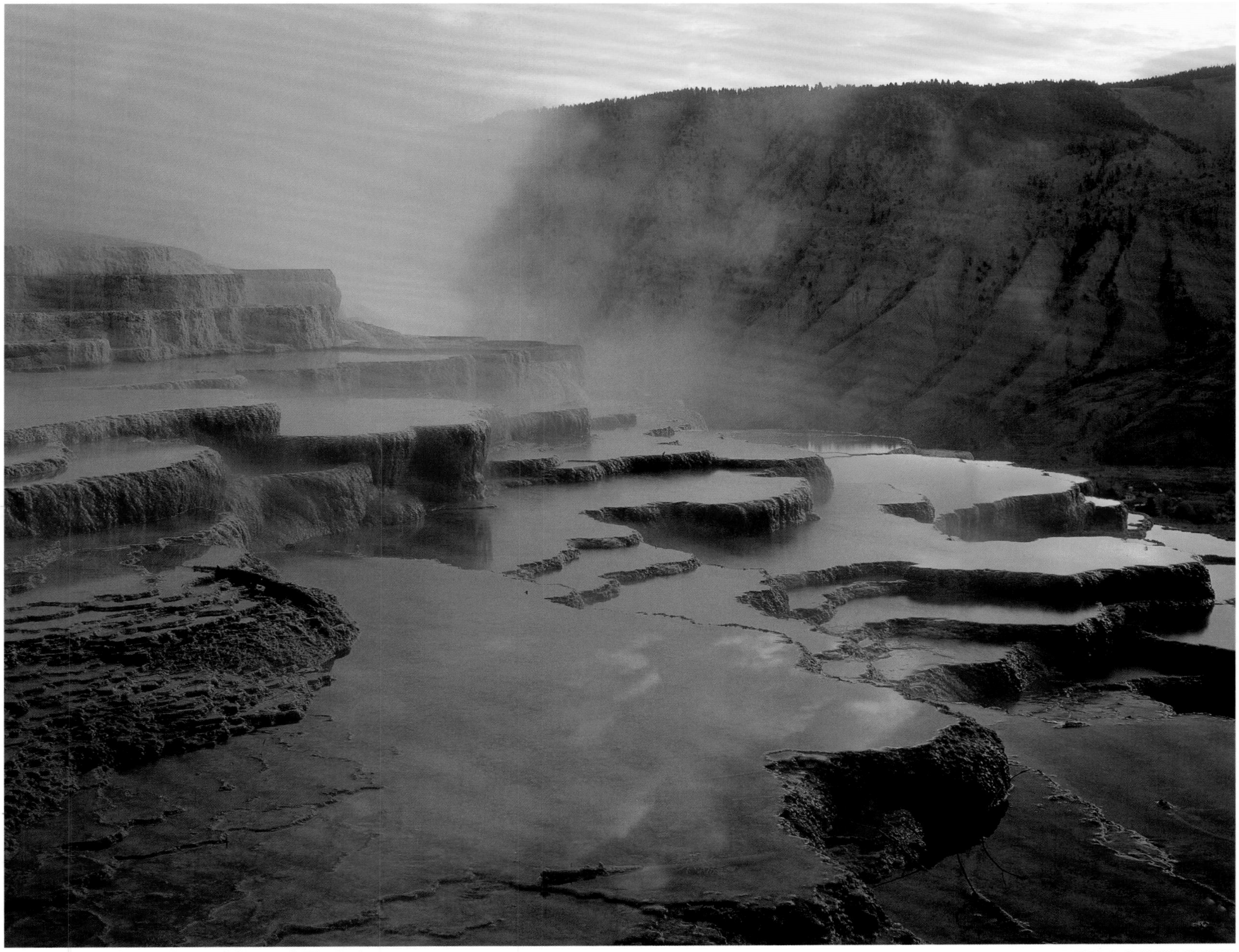

Rising mists at Canary Spring, Mammoth Hot Springs.

wonderland; among the mental images I conjure at the mention of this place. Still, to believe that they are the essence of Yellowstone is to deny the small things, the obscure, or ordinary their fair share of the limelight. Here too, there are enough sights, sounds, odors, and feelings to surfeit my senses.

Like other people, I am drawn to the spectacular—to things of the Guinness Book of Records variety. Yet, I know that there is beauty, drama, and significance in a rotting log, an owl pellet, and the perfect camber of a robin's wing. A soft summer wind alters the landscape as surely as the grinding of an ice age glacier. The ecological processes taking place in a tiny pond on the Blacktail Deer Plateau are identical to those in Yellowstone Lake. Only the scale is different.

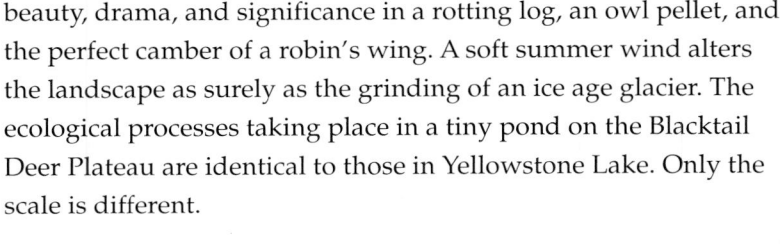

Water lily on Isa Lake.

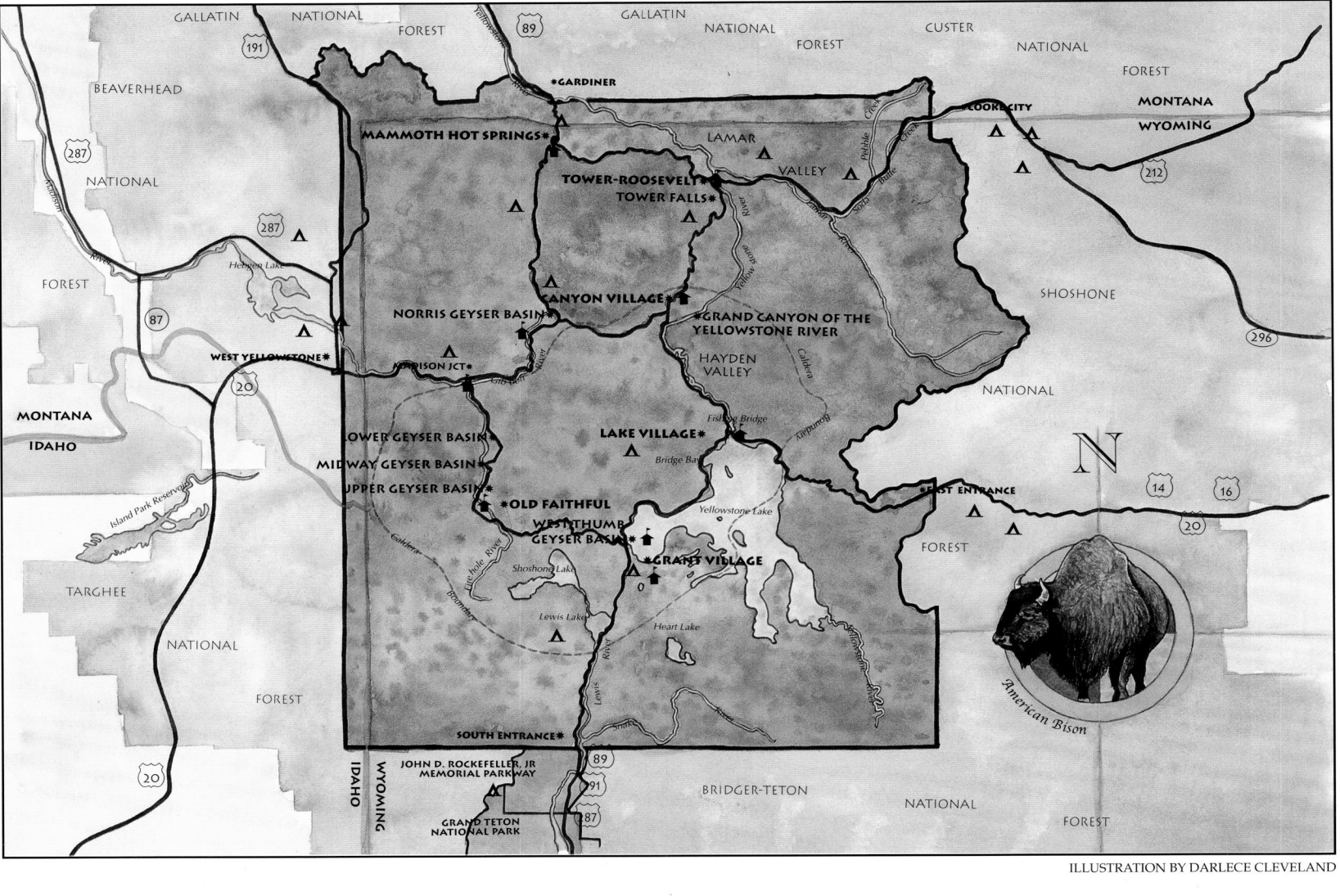

ILLUSTRATION BY DARLECE CLEVELAND

Yellowstone National Park is larger than Rhode Island and Delaware combined. It lies partially in the states of Montana and Idaho, but the largest part of the park is in the northwest corner of Wyoming.

Visitors have the option of entering the park at all of the cardinal points of the compass, plus one. From the north through Gardiner, Montana; from the northeast through Silver Gate and Cooke City, Montana; from the west through West Yellowstone, Montana; from the east, through Cody, Wyoming and the Wapiti Valley; and from the south, through Jackson, Wyoming, Grand Teton National Park, and the John D. Rockefeller Parkway.

At each entrance, park rangers greet visitors, collect fees, and distribute maps and guides. There are nine visitor centers and/or museums with information desks, exhibits, audiovisual programs, and bookstores featuring theme-related interpretive materials. They are located at Mammoth Hot Springs, Norris Geyser Basin, the Museum of the National Park Ranger at Norris, Madison, Canyon, Old Faithful, Grant Village, West Thumb, and Fishing Bridge.

To learn more about Yellowstone, check out the exhibits at visitor centers, or participate in an interpretive program. The National Park Service makes guided walks, campfire programs, demonstrations, and other activities available free of charge. Interpretive activities are available for people of all ages. They are your chance to get to know Yellowstone better.

There are 12 campgrounds in the park. The National Park Service on a first-come, first-served basis operates seven campgrounds totaling 457 campsites. Five, with a total of 1,747 sites, are run by concession and available by reservation only.

Hotels, restaurants, gift shops, service stations, stores, and marinas are operated by park concessions. It is a good idea to make reservations well in advance of your visit—a year is not too early!

The park's 310 miles of paved roads make it possible to easily visit the principal park features and developed areas. For those with the time, and inclination, to visit the amazing Yellowstone backcountry—to seldom-visited places like Thorofare, Cascade Corner, Hoodoo Basin—there are at least 1,000 miles of trails.

Most park roads are closed to automobiles during the winter, but some are groomed for travel in over-snow vehicles. (Note: a restriction on snowmobile access is proposed for the future. Check for information at visitor service desks in concession facilities, or at visitor centers). If you prefer to ski, several fine cross-country ski trails are maintained.

HUMAN HISTORY

Yellowstone country has attracted people for thousands of years. The presence of artifacts confirms periodic human occupation in the region by various cultures for more than 10,000 years. For the last few hundred years the record is fairly complete, yet ample evidence from earlier periods tells us the Yellowstone region was periodically inhabited by Ice Age hunters.

Members of several American Indian tribes are known to have entered Yellowstone during the past 200 years, especially after they acquired the horse from Spanish colonists. Among the tribes that have connections with the area are the Blackfoot, Crow, Shoshone-Bannock, and the Nez Perce, who passed through the park during the final sad flight of Chief Joseph and his band in 1877. In addition to material evidence such as rock tipi rings and brush wickiups, their presence is documented in the journals of early mountain men and explorers such as Jim Bridger, Osborne Russell, and members of the Washburn-Langford expedition.

The Bannocks were a group of northern Paiute living peacefully among the Shoshone. One of the prominent travel routes across Yellowstone Country is the famous Bannock Trail, which was used by the Bannocks and others as they sought bison on the eastern high plains, following the extermination of the herds of the Snake River Plains in the 1800s.

The Shoshone referred to individual tribal bands by the principal food of the group. Thus, within the larger tribe, there were Buffalo Eaters, Salmon Eaters, Rabbit Eaters, and Sheep Eaters. The Sheep Eaters were the only long-term Indian residents in the park.

Sheep Eaters, probably no more than 400 altogether, in 15 camp groups, were first reported in the area by trappers and explorers about 1800. They probably arrived in the park as part of the slow, general migration of tribes across the Great Basin toward the northeast. They lived in the region for only about a hun-

Artist Thomas Moran on Mammoth Terraces. Photograph by William Henry Jackson, 1871.

dred years. They moved their small encampments from high in the mountains in the summer to the lower elevations in winter, adjusting to the seasonal movements of bighorn sheep and the availability of other foods such as small game, berries, nuts, fish, plant roots, ants, and grubs.

Sheep Eater homes were either simple domed wickiups made of loosely stacked poles and brush, covered with animal hides, or were roofless shelters made of a semicircle of poles with branches piled against them. They used rocks, the hand-shaped *mano* and flat *metate*, to grind seeds and nuts into a kind of flour that they mixed and cooked in stone pots. Heavy and cumbersome, the stone implements were often left in the campsite, cached for future use. The Sheep Eaters' clothing was made of soft, finely tanned hides of deer, elk, and bighorn sheep. They used stone knives, scrapers, fire-hardened digging sticks, and made highly prized bows from animal horns and antlers. Hides and horn bows were sometimes traded with other tribes. They hunted mountain sheep with bows and arrows and by constructing traps to capture several animals at a time. By 1882, most of the Sheep Eaters had gone to various reservations because of treaties that excluded them and other tribes from the newly created park.

While some native people may have avoided the more active geothermal features, evidence doesn't indicate that Indians were fearful of these areas. In fact, campsites have been found near some of them. There are indications that they may have believed that the "steaming waters that go up and down" were manifestations of powerful spirits (neither good nor bad) that could be summoned to their aid by prayer. Warriors may have sought them on vision quests. In any case, there is no reason to believe that these first visitors were any more, or less, awed by the geysers and other features than visitors are today.

French Canadian trappers of the 18th century wandered through much of the intermountain West, but they are not known to have seen the thermal features. They did travel the reaches of the upper Missouri

River and its tributaries, including a river that they called the "Roche Jaune," Yellowstone. That watercourse, its headwaters high in the northern Rockies, was to become the namesake for the future park.

John Colter, a mountain man and trapper who had been with the Lewis and Clark Expedition in 1806, was probably the first white man to see the steamy, boiling water and mud, when he ventured into the Yellowstone high country in the winter of 1807-1808. Upon his return to St. Louis three years later, his accounts of the wonders that he had seen were discounted. Assuming the place he described was mythical, a journalist of the time called it "Colter's Hell."

Colter was followed into the region by other hardy mountain men, among them Joe Meek and Jim Bridger, who spent three years trapping in Yellowstone Country. When Bridger returned to St. Louis with tales of a "place where Hell bubbled up," his stories were labeled "preposterous." While he probably embellished a bit, as storytelling mountain men were wont to do, his descriptions of places like Obsidian Cliff, Alum Creek, the Firehole River, and other landmarks were not so far-fetched.

The trappers were followed, in the 1860s, by people driven by commerce of a different sort. Prospectors, caught up in the frenzy over the rich Montana gold strike of 1862, entered the area but found none of the alluring metal. In 1865, one of them, Walter W. De Lacy, published the first relatively accurate map of the region.

Determined to see for themselves the wonders described by others, local residents David E. Folsom, Charles W. Cook, and William Peterson entered the area in 1869. They saw most of what Colter, Bridger, and De Lacy had seen—and much more. They explored extensively and produced a much improved version of De Lacy's 1865 map. Their exploits were recounted in newspapers and in an article for the Chicago magazine, *Western Monthly*.

In 1870, a larger expedition that included

Visitors at Mammoth Hot Springs, 1958.

several prominent residents of the Montana Territory was mounted. It was led by the surveyor general Henry D. Washburn. Washburn was accompanied by Nathaniel P. Langford (later to become the first superintendent of the new park), lawyer Cornelius Hedges, and Truman Everts, along with a military escort under the command of Lieutenant Gustavus C. Doane.

The growing publicity finally resulted in the United States government funding and supporting an official exploration in 1871. The large expedition was led by Ferdinand V. Hayden, head of the U.S. Geological Survey. Hayden's purpose was to explore the region thoroughly and scientifically, and it was complemented by a simultaneous survey by the U.S. Army Corps of Engineers. A stunning and convincing visual record was created by noted photographer William Henry Jackson and by artists Henry W. Elliott and Thomas Moran.

Members of these expeditions were so impressed by the spectacle of the place they became convinced that it should somehow be reserved for others to see and enjoy. In 1871 and early 1872, Hayden and members of the Washburn party and others lobbied tirelessly for a congressional bill to protect Yellowstone for the benefit of everyone. Supported by the impressive imagery of Jackson, Moran, and Elliot, and following the precedent of the 1864 Yosemite Land Grant Act that made Yosemite Valley part of the public domain, Congress enacted historic legislation. Yellowstone was officially designated the world's first national park when President Ulysses S. Grant signed the bill on March 1, 1872.

In 1886, following years of underfunded, disorganized, ineffective management, the park was officially entrusted to the care of the U. S. Army. During the ensuing 30 years, army custodians accomplished much. They improved access to the park, constructed facilities (some of which are still in use), protected its features, and made early visitors more secure.

THE GEYSER BASINS:

Terraced pools, Great Fountain Geyser, sunset.   PHOTO © RANDI HIRSCHMANN

A few columns and puffs of steam are seen rising above the
tree-tops… indicating geysers and hot springs, gentle-looking
and noiseless as downy clouds, softly hinting the reaction
going on between the surface and the hot interior.
— John Muir, *Yellowstone National Park*

Hot water collects in small pools near the vent and drains outward in multicolored channels across the low mound of pastel earth. At the center, evanescent wisps of steam issue from the ground, and hover wraithlike in the sulphurous air. A deep sound emanates with increasing volume from the sunless throat. At Nature's appointed time, a column of superheated steam and water flashes upward from the ground, higher, then higher, until it hangs momentarily suspended like iridescent crystalline statuary. Then, it collapses, and is drawn back into the ground. Predictably, the earth will expel another hot, Plutonian breath in another hour or so. Thus, the clepsydra-like repetitious spectacle of Old Faithful continues.

Nowhere else in the world is there a greater array of geothermal features than in Yellowstone—more than 10,000 known to date. More than half of the world's geysers—perhaps 200 to 250 of them, including the largest and tallest on earth—are here. Most of the geysers and other geothermal features are gathered into areas called basins. These sulphurous communities of hot water, steam, bubbling mud, and primitive life forms are all located within or near the rim of the huge crater that marks the volcanic womb of the park.

While their working parts are similar, each geyser has a specific gestation period, distinctive form, and behavior. No two are alike, and their inconstant behavior is a reflection of the constancy of change in Yellowstone.

Each of Yellowstone's geysers has a distinct personality. Some of Old Faithful's supporting cast on the Yellowstone stage are quieter and more reserved. Others are more demonstrative. But all follow the same script and have a common director—an interconnected underground plumbing system. Only their performances are different.

All but Lone Star, Shoshone, and Heart Lake Basins are easily accessible from park roads. While their relative isolation helps insulate them from the impact of millions of people, visiting the more remote basins can be a wonderfully serendipitous adventure for those who have the time to venture into the backcountry.

The Upper Basin is the most populous geyser community. In addition to Old Faithful, more than 130 geysers and many colorful hot springs reside here. Among Old Faithful's neighbors are Beehive, Grand, Riverside, Giantess, and Castle Geysers.

Farther north, just below Madison Junction, lies the Lower Geyser Basin. It is the second largest basin, the home of Great Fountain and Imperial Geysers and the curious and odorous Fountain Paint Pot.

The oldest, most active, and most frequently changing basin is Norris. It lies above the intersection of two major faults: one extending south from Mammoth and one reaching east from Hebgen Lake. They, in turn, are joined by other fractures that extend outward from the rim of the caldera. It is a busy subterranean intersection where earth-moving adjustments are continually being made. The features of Norris have been changing in response to tremors originating along these faults for about 115,000 years.

In addition, Norris is the hottest thermal basin, with a temperature of 459°F, a little more than 1,000 feet beneath the surface. It is also the location of Steamboat Geyser, the tallest, and possibly the most unpredictable geyser in the world. Eruptions from Bead Geyser, only 15 to 25 feet in height, seldom vary more than 30 seconds from the average frequency. It is the most regular of all the geysers. Although Old Faithful is the single feature most often associated with Yellowstone, it is neither the oldest, tallest, hottest, nor the most regular geyser.

Sinter is an opalescent substance that is deposited by geysers and other thermal features, building the distinctive geothermal landforms in geyser basins. It is a material that has been dissolved by hot water seeping through the deep, silica-rich rocks that cover

---

OPPOSITE: White Dome Geyser, moonlit eruption, Lower Geyser Basin. PHOTO © MICHAEL FRYE

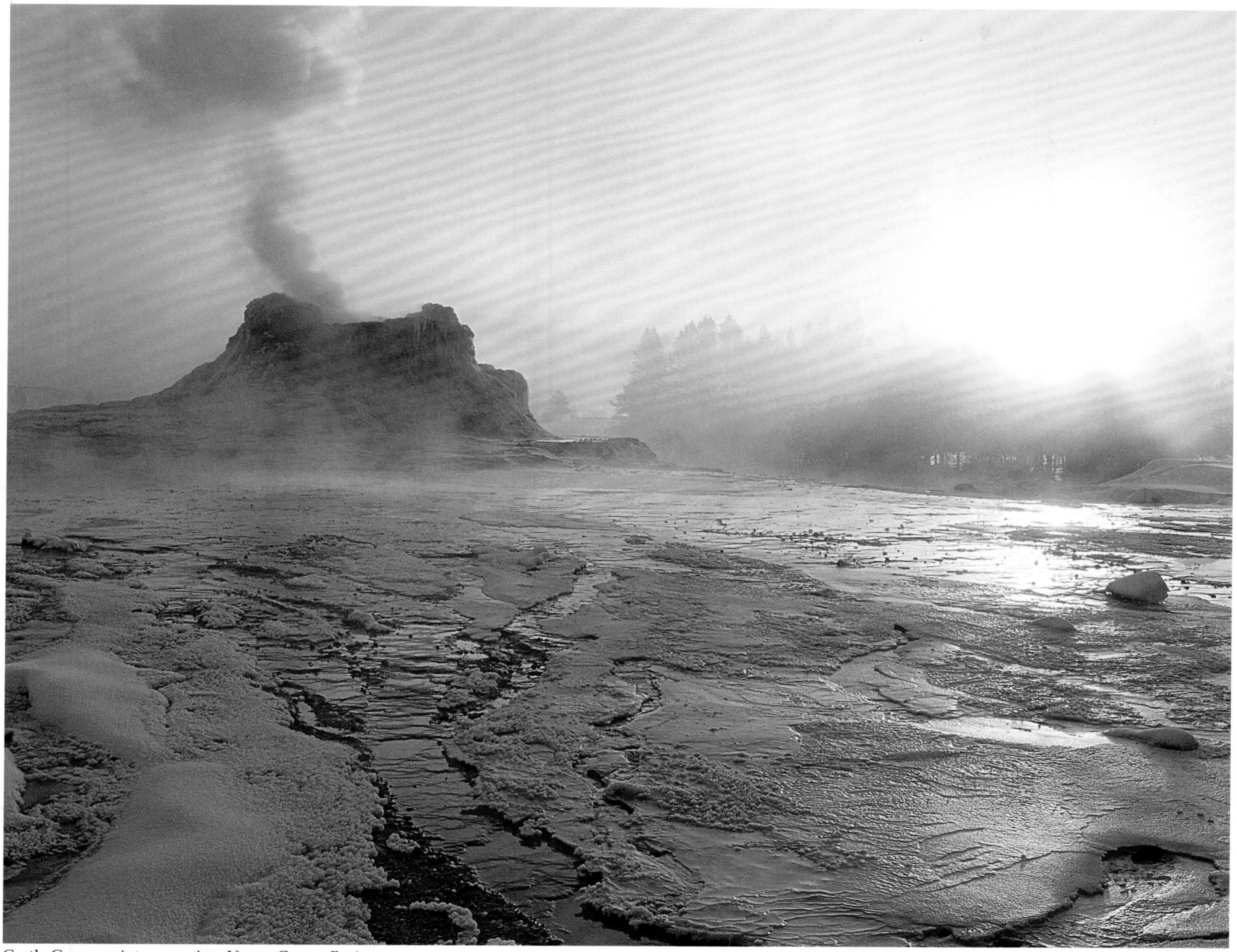

Castle Geyser, winter eruption, Upper Geyser Basin. PHOTO © JEFF VANUGA

much of the central plateau and redeposited on the surface as the waters cool.

Thermal basins are works in progress, constantly changing colors and textures. The canvas—the background color—is a muted, whitish-gray that stands out against the dark green surrounding forest. Its colors mainly come from the powdery sinter that coats it, highlighted by kaleidoscopic accents of mineral greens, blues, and yellows. The blues in sunlight are reflected back causing the hot water to appear emerald, and deceptively cool as if in a mountain lake. The brimstone yellows come from sulphur, and colonial thermophilic algae add hues of red, orange, and brown to the veinlike channels of water radiating from thermal features, depending on water temperature.

Standing in the swirling sulphurous mist in Norris Geyser Basin, I imagine myself in a prehistoric world, where tiny heat-tolerant organisms are among the first living things on the young planet earth.

Erupting mudpot near Mud Volcano. PHOTO © FRED HIRSCHMANN

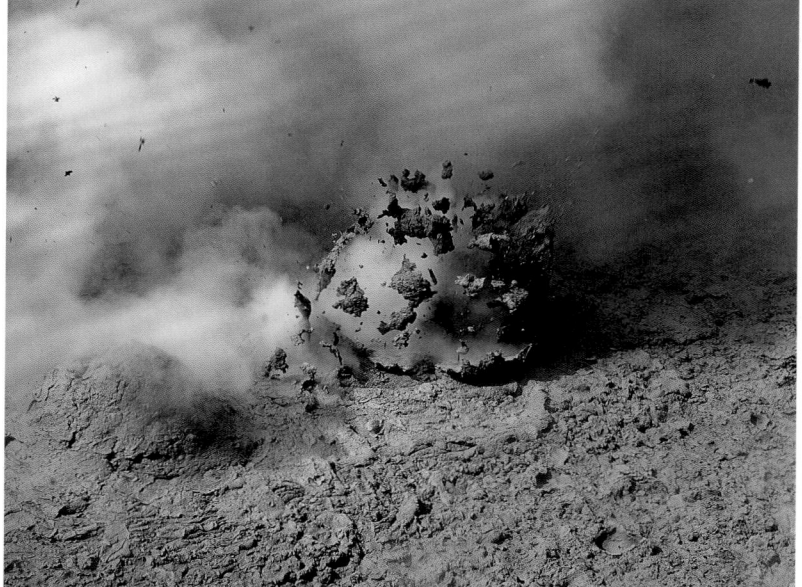

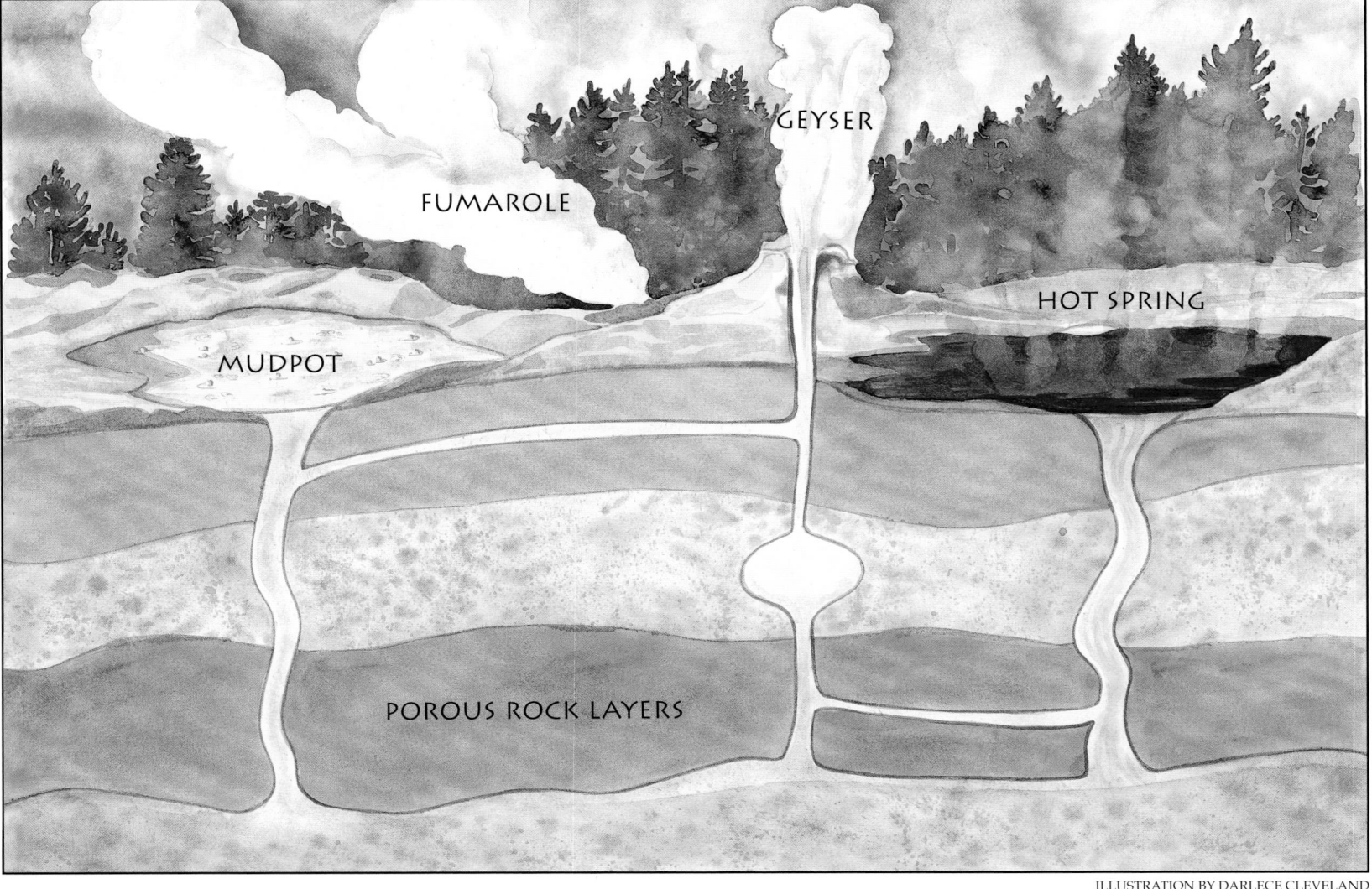

FUMAROLE

GEYSER

HOT SPRING

MUDPOT

POROUS ROCK LAYERS

ILLUSTRATION BY DARLECE CLEVELAND

The list of materials needed for Nature to fashion a geothermal feature is brief: an ample and constant supply of water, a system of subterranean reservoirs and pathways, and a source of heat. All of the ingredients are in ample supply on this high volcanic plateau. Draped across the Continental Divide, Yellowstone is among the first places to receive runoff from summer storms, and winter brings deep snow that, in the spring, melts to add to the water supply. Each year, precipitation varies from 10 inches or so at the lowest points to 80 inches in the higher country. Heat is provided by molten rock, closer to the surface here than in most other parts of the world, and possibly by the radioactive decay of elements very deep in the earth's mantle. The ring fracturing that foreshadowed the collapse of the Yellowstone Caldera created an underground network of fault lines and fractures. Spaces in otherwise solid rock al-

low gravity to draw cold water down thousands of feet, where it collects, is heated to high temperature, and eventually returns to the surface in forms both sublime and subtle.

As the water is heated, temperatures rise well above the boiling point—to 400 degrees or more. Still, this superheated water remains liquid because of the great pressure and weight pushing down on it from overlying rock and water. The hot water is less dense than the colder, heavier water percolating downward around it. Following a network of cracks and fissures in the rock, lighter, more buoyant, superheated water slowly moves toward the surface. When extremely hot water nears the surface, the pressure exerted over the water lessens, and what began as rain and snowmelt reappears in different garb.

When water is gradually released, a hot spring is formed. Fumaroles (steam vents) develop when

water boils away before reaching the surface. If sulphuric acid is present, rock surrounding the vent is dissolved, mixes with water, and forms bubbling mudpots. Where hot water rises through limestone, it slowly flows across the surface, building terraces of a material called travertine. Expanding steam building up behind a constriction in the plumbing system eventually pushes through the conduit, forcing overlying water to overflow from the vent. This drops the pressure on the superheated water below, which flashes into steam as the water rapidly expands, and a geyser is born.

GEOLOGIC HISTORY

This region's geologic past is long and varied, with the oldest rocks in Yellowstone—pinkish, crystalline granites, dark-banded gneisses, and schists of the Precambrian Era—dating back 2.7 billion years. During the intervening eons, Nature's reconstructive surgery has altered the face of the ancient landscape many times.

Five hundred million years ago, the land was covered by shallow inland seas in which vast quantities of calcium carbonate, sand, and mud collected to form thick layers of sediment that eventually hardened under the pressure of overlying layers into strata of limestone, sandstone, and shale. This period of sedimentation and rock formation occurred when North America was just a small part of a single, enormous continent.

Yellowstone rides on a giant tectonic plate, a piece of the earth's crust floating here and there on convection currents in the molten upper mantle. This tectonic plate, known as the North American Plate, is a remnant of a huge primordial single land mass called Pangaea. That giant continent broke apart about 300 million years ago, setting its pieces adrift on a hot, planetary lake, and causing Yellowstone to begin its long voyage toward the hot tip of a stationary plume of molten rock far to the west.

About 100 to 50 million years ago powerful mountain-building activity—the result of a massive collision between the North American Plate and the Pacific Plate—folded, faulted, and compressed the earth, eventually uplifting it to form the Rocky Mountains.

As the Rocky Mountain uplift came to a close about 50 million years ago, a 15-million-year period of volcanic eruptions began. The Absaroka and Washburn Mountains that border the central plateau on the east and the west of Yellowstone were born during this long, volcanic episode. The chain of mountains vomited huge quantities of silica-rich lava and ash. The ejected material mixed with water to form mudflows that swept down slope, burying standing forests of redwoods, sycamores, magnolias, dogwoods, and other trees that had established themselves in climatic conditions very different from today. Many of these ancient trees of stone—the largest petrified forest in the world—now cover Specimen Ridge and other slopes above Lamar Valley.

During the last two million years, successive advances of glacial ice have sculpted the older Yellowstone landscape. The most recent period of glaciation began about 50,000 years ago, during a period of global cooling. In the Absaroka-Beartooth Wilderness, northeast of the park, deep perennial snow gradually transformed into ice, which thickened into frigid sheets thousands of feet thick.

Driven by their own weight, mountain glaciers flowed down valleys and out over the central plateau, where they converged into a vast ice field that covered the park. For thousands of years, ice flowed outward from this immense ice field, leaving behind ample evidence of its passage. U-shaped valleys, glacial moraine deposits, polished and striated rock, and erratics, or boulders incongruously dropped miles away from distant mountains—all are the work of glacial ice. During this chilling time, which ended about 15,000 years ago, only the highest mountaintops appeared like islands in a boundless sea of ice.

Yellowstone is an avatar of the incredible power of geologic process. It is a landscape that has been roughly shaped by mountain building and volcanic eruptions and finely detailed by glacial ice. On at least three occasions, about 600,000 years apart, gigantic eruptions eviscerated the central plateau. Each eruption was a prodigious explosive display of the latent energy of volcanic material accumulating in shallow pockets beneath the park. The same energy gave birth to and continues to fuel the myriad geothermal features for which Yellowstone is famous.

Hot spots jut upward through the earth's continental crust in numerous places, most often they are found on the thin ocean floor (the Hawaiian Islands, for example, continue to be formed by hot spot activity). The continental land mass overlying the earth's mantle is much thicker—perhaps 30 miles deep—yet in Yellowstone a plume of magma (molten rock) rises through the mantle into the crust to within a couple of miles of the surface. This hotspot remains stationary as the North American continent drifts over it as if moving over the flame of a welder's torch.

A trail of older calderas extends beyond Yellowstone to the southwest, confirming the gradual southwesterly migration of the continent in relation to the hotspot. Over a short span of geologic time, three prodigious eruptions tied to the hot spot collectively ejected more than 900 cubic miles of volcanic debris from the Yellowstone region—mostly ash particles welded together by intense heat into a rock called welded tuff.

About two million years ago, the hot spot forced part of Idaho's Snake River Plain upward in an expanding dome of magma, thinly covered by layers of rock that ultimately fractured, releasing what is considered one of the largest volcanic eruption in the history of the earth. About 1.3 million years ago, just outside the park's southwest boundary, in the area called Island Park, the Yellowstone hotspot fueled another, though smaller, eruption.

Then, about 630,000 years ago, the shape of Yellowstone was dramatically altered in an event that dominates its recent geologic history. Molten rock rising from beneath the hotspot accumulated near the surface in a mushroomlike reservoir. **1.** As the mass of molten rock grew larger, digesting more and more of the rock beneath the central plateau, the thin ground above it arched upward in a broad dome. Eventually, stretched belly-tight, a series of concentric cracks formed around the edge of the dome. **2.** These cracks, or ring fractures, spread downward until they breached the highly pressurized chamber, resulting in the sudden, catastrophic release of more than 240 cubic miles of gas, molten rock, and

ABOVE: Lichen encrusted Sheepeater Cliffs. PHOTO © JEFF FOOTT

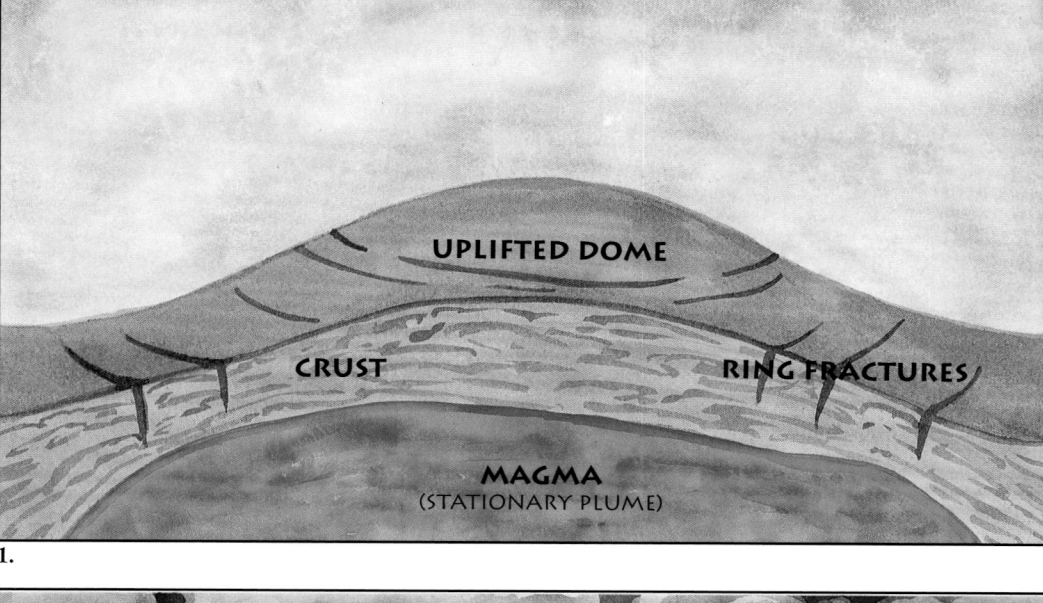

1.

2.

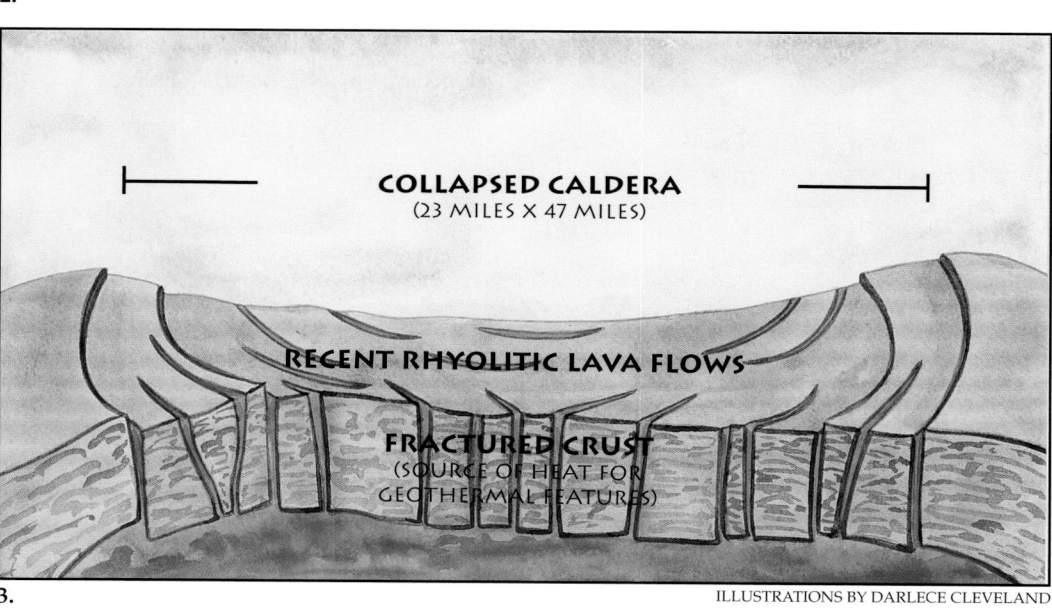

3.

ILLUSTRATIONS BY DARLECE CLEVELAND

ash—an explosion that may have been 1,000 times more powerful than the Mount Saint Helens eruption in 1980.

Incendiary volcanic ash vented from the ring fractures at temperatures in excess of 1,500°F. A swiftly spreading cloud of ash darkened the sky and fell across thousands of square miles. That deadly swarm incinerated every living thing in the region and probably altered the world's climate and weather for years.

3. As volcanic debris vacated the magma chamber there was nothing left to support its roof, and it collapsed in on itself along the ring fractures, creating a giant caldera several thousand feet deep. Either the eruption or the subsequent collapse of the chamber consumed the mountains and other surface features in the greater part of Yellowstone. The caldera is immense, measuring approximately 47 miles long and 23 miles wide. Following the collapse, intermittent lava flows quietly and slowly spread into the immense crater, filling much of it in so that the caldera rim is largely obscured. Lava continued to flow until about 70,000 years ago, gradually building the Yellowstone plateau in the void where the crater had been.

Today, the floor of the caldera is bulging upward. This may be both a confirmation of the fixed nature of the hot spot, and an indication of another volcanic event in Yellowstone's future. Located beneath the north end of Yellowstone Lake, the shallow dome is believed to overlie a reservoir of molten rock that is growing measurably larger, as it is filled through the fiery conduit to the earth's mantle. The uplift has formed LeHardy Rapids on the Yellowstone River, which is considered the true outlet of Yellowstone Lake. Evidence also suggests that the lakebed itself is tilting gradually to the southwest. If this uplift continues in the future, Yellowstone Lake may no longer drain to the north via the Yellowstone and Missouri Rivers but rather to the south, via the Snake and Columbia Rivers, ultimately reaching the Pacific.

A visit to Yellowstone allows you to descend into the one of the largest volcanic craters on Earth, yet one that may be dwarfed in size in the future.

PAGE 28 & 29: Elk in the Firehole River near Biscuit Basin, Upper Geyser Basin, winter morning. PHOTO © JEFF HENRY

Aprons of colorful algae at Grand Prismatic Spring, Midway Geyser Basin.

The Firehole River's Upper Basin is the most populous and popular geyser community. It is the home of Old Faithful, undoubtedly the best known, if not the most regular, geyser in the world. Altogether, more than 150 geysers and many colorful hot springs are concentrated into about one square mile in this famous valley.

While most geysers erupt at the whim of Nature, Old Faithful and some of its more predictable kin—Daisy, Grand, Riverside, and Castle Geysers in the Upper Basin—keep to a fairly regular schedule. All of them are formed in a generally similar way but what distinguishes them is the different ways that they erupt. Old Faithful jets straight upward in its unmistakable column of iridescent water and steam. Riverside Geyser shoots at an angle across the Firehole River, as it consistently has since its discovery in 1871. Grand Geyser erupts in a series of timpanilike explo-

sions. Appropriately named by a member of the Washburn Expedition, Castle Geyser vents from a cone that looks like the parapet of a medieval fortress. Elsewhere, Punch Bowl Spring, with its low, scalloped edge, looks like a miniature caldera filled with a lake of boiling water continuously shrouded in steam.

The Firehole River, which originates south of Old Faithful, flows through the Upper Geyser Basin, on to the Midway and Lower Basins, and eventually to its confluence with the Gibbon River at Madison Junction. Midway Geyser Basin is the home of spectacularly colored Grand Prismatic Spring. The noisy bubbling mud of Fountain Paint Pot identifies the Lower Geyser Basin, where each of the different types of geothermal features in the park may be seen. Between the two basins, Firehole Lake Drive passes by Great Fountain Geyser.

The river is born in cold springs on the Madison Plateau, then falls over the 125-foot Kepler Cascades before reaching the Upper Geyser Basin. It was dubbed "Firehole" by early trappers in the area who saw all the steam rising from the thermal features surrounding the river and thought it was smoke from fires. The term for a mountain valley in mountain man parlance was hole. Thus the river was named. While it is not fire-hot, the temperature of river water is measurably elevated by runoff from the many geysers and springs in the basin. Where hot water drains into the river, perpetual but evanescent clouds of steam hover overhead.

OPPOSITE: Old Faithful Geyser, winter morning eruption, Upper Geyser Basin.

Blue Geyser erupting in Porcelain Basin.

PHOTO © FRED HIRSCHMANN

The oldest, most active, and most frequently changing basin is Norris. It was named for Philetus W. Norris, the second superintendent of Yellowstone, who provided the first detailed information about the thermal features. Norris Geyser Basin is the hottest, oldest, and most changeable of Yellowstone's thermal areas. The features in the basin change often, with frequent disturbances from seismic activity and water fluctuations.

Norris is the location of Steamboat Geyser, the tallest, and possibly the most unpredictable geyser in the world. Perhaps no other geyser is more indicative of the variability of eruptive cycles—from four days to 50 years. Until May 2, 2000, Steamboat had not erupted for nine years, yet during the 1980s it erupted 23 times in one summer.

Norris sits above a busy subterranean intersection where earth-moving adjustments are continually being made. The Norris–Mammoth Corridor is a fault that runs from Norris north through Mammoth to the Gardiner, Montana, area. The Hebgen Lake fault runs from northwest of West Yellowstone, Montana, to Norris. These two faults intersect with a ring fracture formed during the collapse of the Yellowstone caldera. These active faults are the primary reason that Norris Geyser Basin is so hot and dynamic.

The highest temperature ever recorded in a geothermal area—459°F at 1,087 feet—was measured at Norris (there are very few thermal features under the boiling point—199°F at this elevation). Most of the waters at Norris are acidic, including rare acid geysers, like Echinus.

Three smaller basins are contained within Norris Geyser Basin: Porcelain Basin, Back Basin, and One Hundred Springs Plain. Porcelain Basin is largely barren of trees, and there are more geothermic features concentrated there. Back Basin is more heavily wooded, with features scattered throughout the area. One Hundred Springs Plain is an off-trail section of the Norris Geyser Basin that is very acidic. Only a thin crust that cannot support much weight covers much of the ground. It is very dangerous to travel here without the guidance of a park ranger.

Norris is a good place to observe life in the harsh conditions of a geyser basin. Runoff channels tinted by heat-tolerant organisms form colorful threads of water that extend from a geyser's mouth like strands in a web. Tiny brine flies flit about among algal mats in the in-between world of runoff channels—residents of neither earth nor sky. Killdeer feed on the ephydrid flies and lay their eggs on the bare warm ground.

OPPOSITE: Steamboat Geyser—the world's tallest, seen during a rare eruption. PHOTO © FRED HIRSCHMANN

Bull elk with harem, Mammoth Hot Springs.

PHOTO © JEFF FOOTT

The spectacular crenellated terraces at Mammoth Hot Springs are the first geothermal features that visitors entering from the north will see; yet they are very different from the others. Unlike the sinter that is common in most geyser basins, the terrace-building material at Mammoth Hot Springs is travertine—a derivative of limestone that underlies the springs.

Hot water charged with carbon dioxide—like carbonated drinks—forms a weak carbonic acid solution. As the acidic water rises through limestone, it dissolves large quantities of the rock, which is made mostly of calcium carbonate. Once the water reaches the ground surface, some of the carbon dioxide escapes, depositing the white, chalky mineral called travertine. About two tons of travertine is deposited each day on the terraces.

The terraces are distinctively different from other geothermal features, but the same ingredients are necessary for their formation—water, heat, and a subterranean plumbing system. Mammoth lies outside the Yellowstone Caldera, but its underground water is heated by the same volcanic source that fuels features within or closer to the crater rim. Geologists believe that hot water flows from Norris to Mammoth along a fault line that more or less parallels the road from Norris to Mammoth. Shallow circulation along this fault allows super-heated water from Norris to cool to about 170° F. before coming to the surface at Mammoth.

There are no geysers at Mammoth Hot Springs, but travertine-producing features like Minerva, Narrow Gauge, and New Highland Springs create many ornate, tiered terraces, some with opaline scalloped edges containing shallow pools of hot water. The constantly evolving terraces make for a colorful backdrop to old Fort Yellowstone.

Terrace Mountain, northwest of Golden Gate, has a thick cap of travertine. The ancient terraces extend from the present location, across the Parade Ground, and down to Boiling River. All of the buildings at Mammoth—the hotel, park headquarters, the visitor center, and others—are built upon an old terrace formation known as Hotel Terrace. Some places beneath the terraces have been eaten away by acidic water. When Fort Yellowstone was constructed in 1891, concern was expressed that the hollow ground would not support the weight of the buildings, but construction proceeded. Evidence of what is called thermal karst topography can be seen in several large sinkholes on the parade ground.

OPPOSITE: Minerva Terrace at Mammoth Hot Springs. PHOTO © DICK DIETRICH

WEST THUMB GEYSER BASIN

Hot spring and steam vent at West Thumb Geyser Basin.

West Thumb Geyser Basin, including Potts Basin to the north, is the largest geyser basin on the shores of Yellowstone Lake. With the deep blue water of the West Thumb embayment as a backdrop, the basin is one of the most picturesque in the park. The thermal features here are not limited to the lakeshore, but also extend under the surface of the lake. Recently, scientists have discovered vast fields of geothermally created spires on the bottom of West Thumb Bay and other parts of Yellowstone Lake. During the winter, the presence of some of these submarine features is disclosed by melt holes in the icy surface of the lake. River otters are commonly seen along the thermally melted areas of the lake during the winter months, where they harvest fish. Sometimes opportunistic fish thieves like coyotes and ravens join them.

The 1869 Folsom-Cook-Peterson Expedition visited the West Thumb Geyser Basin. Wrote David Folsom:

> "There were several hundred springs here, varying in size from miniature fountains to pools or wells seventy-five feet in diameter and of great depth. The water had a pale violet tinge, and was very clear, enabling us to discern small objects fifty or sixty feet below the surface. A small cluster of mud springs nearby claimed our attention. These were filled with mud, resembling thick paint of the finest quality, differing in color from pure white to the various shades of yellow, pink, red and violet. During the afternoon they threw mud to the height of fifteen feet."

In the past, some visitors traveling to Yellowstone would arrive at West Thumb via stagecoach from the Old Faithful area. At West Thumb, they had the choice of continuing on the dusty, bumpy stagecoach or boarding the steamship *Zillah* to continue the journey by water to the Lake Hotel. The boat dock was located in the south end of the basin, near Lakeside Spring.

Abyss Pool, one of the deepest hot springs in Yellowstone, descends to 53 feet. Comparing it to a jewel, an 1830s visitor called it "a great, pure, sparkling sapphire, rippling with heat." Abyss pool erupted periodically between 1987 and 1992 but has remained placid since that time.

Fishing Cone is a unique hot spring located in the West Thumb Geyser Basin. Some people have said that early anglers caught fish and immediately dipped them into the hot water to prepare an instant meal.

OPPOSITE: Fishing Cone and Lake Yellowstone—dawn from West Thumb. PHOTO © JEFF NICHOLAS

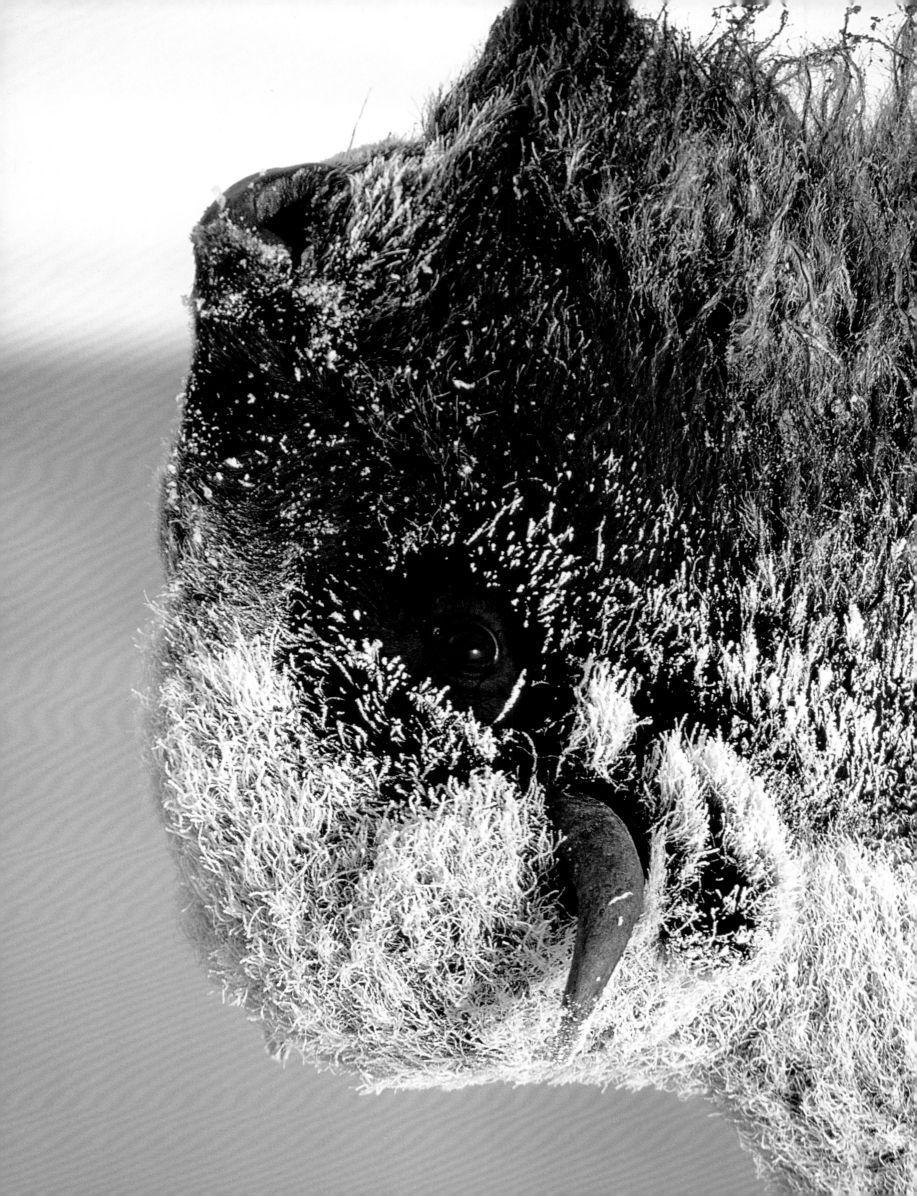

THE
WILDLIFE:

Bighorn sheep ram, sunrise.

Where plays the child
Who will live to see,
The last grizzly roam wild;
The last eagle fly free?
—Keith Bennett, *Untitled*

As I watch a small herd of bison moving through Hayden Valley, glimpse a couple of grizzly bears near Pelican Creek, and observe a few hundred elk grazing the northern range, I tell myself, "This is what primitive wild America was like." The difference is that thousands more of these creatures ranged freely across western North America when it was known only to indigenous peoples— and I am saddened by what we have lost. As available living space has dwindled, places like Yellowstone have become the last refuges for many wild plants and animals.

All organisms are eating or being eaten; processing food. Plants and animals are connected through intricate natural processes such as food chains and predator-prey relationships through which energy is transferred from one trophic level to the next. Some are producers; others are consumers; still others are decomposers that begin new life with each death. And, true to the protocols of Nature, there are always fewer individuals at higher levels in a food chain. My binoculars track a distant grizzly bear across a slope in the Antelope Creek drainage, and I am reminded that in its 600 pounds of bone, muscle, and tendon is concentrated the energy of millions of pine nuts, berries, and ants; thousands of pocket gophers and voles; hundreds of cutthroat trout; and, tens of bison and elk calves.

In midwinter, I see a bison sweeping its giant head from side to side on the ground, stirring up a cloud of white powder, as it attempts to find living plants beneath deep snow. In late summer I discover a pika's miniature haystack of harvested grass hidden away on a talus slope. In spring, I watch sandhill cranes and white pelicans return from lower latitudes. In mid- to late-July, ubiquitous Uintah ground squirrels seem to disappear at once, only to suddenly reappear again in March. In the geyser basins, I see the multicolored hues in runoff channels caused by photosynthetic blue-green bacteria, and I am reminded that all creatures are adapted to extremes of weather and climate.

In few other places in North America is it possible to experience the richness of environments and wildlife of pre-Columbian North America. In just a few hours I can travel from country sparsely covered with sage and cactus near Mammoth Hot Springs, through forests of Douglas fir, lodgepole pine, and spruce, up to frigid, windswept barrens above timberline.

I can walk among tall, 400-year-old fir trees, step into a fire-created forest of lodgepole pine saplings early in their lives, or admire the wind-sculpted contortions of an ancient whitebark pine. In the harsh, seemingly inhospitable world near the summit of the highest peaks I marvel at the resolute endurance of life in the alpine tundra. Like skilled and persistent climbers, lichen cling to rocks like rough, weathered skin, and low-growing plants like moss campion and mountain avens eke out an existence in a place where few animals but birds survive. I can stand in a luxuriant meadow, peppered with fragrant and colorful spring wildflowers, watch trout laboring against the current at LeHardy Rapids, and listen to loons on Peale Island. In short order, I can see large numbers of all of the native North American wild ungulates, hundreds of birds and small mammals, and maybe even a bear or two. I imagine Yellowstone to be like parts of Africa. The Lamar Valley—heart of what wildlife managers call the Northern Range—reminds me of scenes of the Serengeti Plain in East Africa.

But, it is not the richness that is important—there are many more species of animals on the Serengeti; greater diversity of plant and animal life in a tropical rain forest. Rather, it is the integrity of Yellowstone's living community that is most significant. It is virtually unaltered from the time of the American Indian and mountain man. A nearly original flora and fauna is rare in a natural world vastly smaller than the

---

OPPOSITE: Ice-crusted bison, mid-winter.

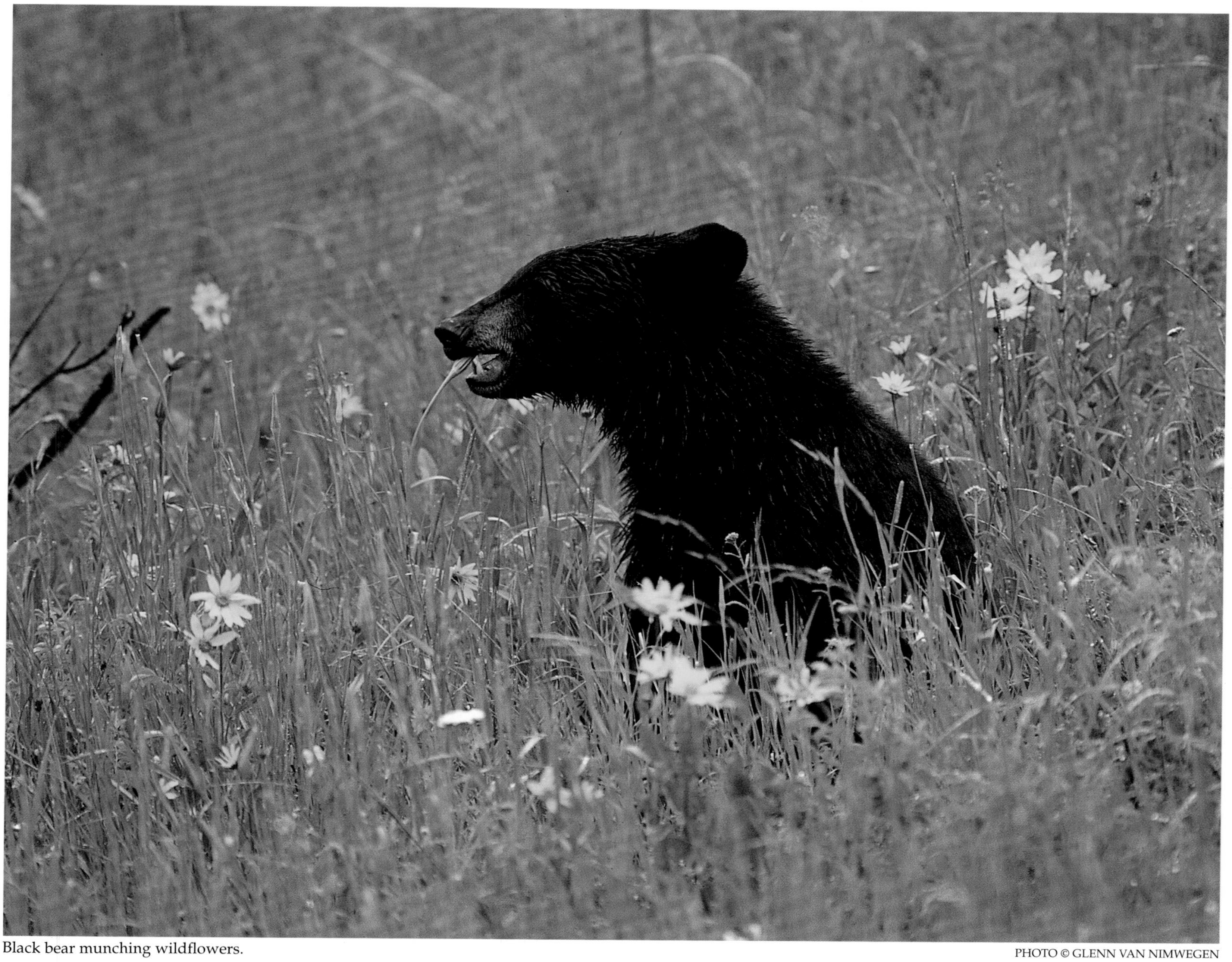

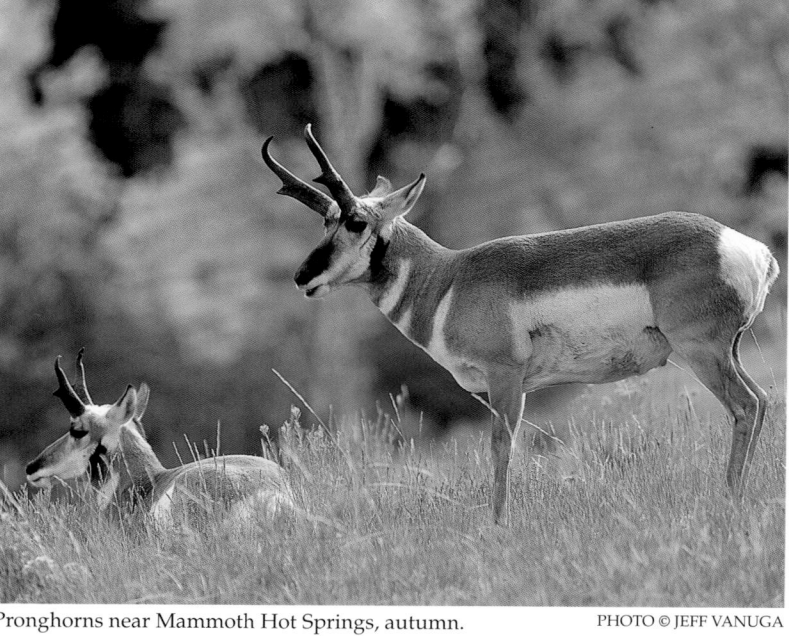

Black bear munching wildflowers. PHOTO © GLENN VAN NIMWEGEN

one people have built. Save for the black-footed ferret, the area is now believed to have a complete native vertebrate fauna, with all of its ecological associations intact. It is a vignette of primitive America and I sometimes imagine myself walking beside John Colter, Jim Bridger, or Osborne Russell, marveling at the diverse and abundant wildlife.

Wildlife and their habitats are under siege. There are more than 40 species of vertebrates, hundreds of invertebrates, and more than 135 plants federally listed as rare, threatened, or endangered. Yellowstone may only be a temporary haven for those vulnerable species near the edge of extinction. Must they be forever lost to the sight of man? I pray not, for their demise would diminish the richness of Yellowstone's living community. There is strength in natural diversity, but the permanent loss of a species weakens the integrity of an ecosystem. I would mourn for my children and grandchildren the death of a species they might never see.

Pronghorns near Mammoth Hot Springs, autumn. PHOTO © JEFF VANUGA

Black bear.   PHOTO © JEFF FOOTT

Grizzly bear.   PHOTO © DIANA STRATTON

BEARS OF YELLOWSTONE

A wild predator is a celebration of death, but when I was 18 and working in grizzly country I was not frightened by bears. I even thought that confronting a predator might be the ultimate wilderness experience. But as I've aged, and witnessed a bear's power to maim and kill, I am no longer able to completely relax in Yellowstone's backcountry. As I have grown older, I've become more conscious of my mortality, and I am now encumbered by a persistent awareness of a potential encounter with a grizzly.

The grizzly bear is the signature animal of Yellowstone. Its population is one of two remaining, relatively large, and self-regulating populations in the lower 48 states. There are good years and bad years, but the grizzly population hovers between 250 to 600 in the Greater Yellowstone Ecosystem. A mature grizzly can range over 1000 square miles in a single season before entering the safe seclusion of winter sleep. Unaware of political boundaries the grizzly frequently passes beyond the park's protection. The grizzly's home range is larger than any North American land mammal, and it is especially vulnerable to habitat loss. The grizzly is omnivorous. It consumes hundreds of pounds of pine nuts, berries, and ants, in addition to pocket gophers, trout, and elk and bison calves.

Years ago, visitors gathered at garbage dumps to watch scores of bears—blacks and grizzlies alike—feast on leftovers, while park naturalists narrated the spectacle. Long lines of automobiles backed up, while hungry bears were fed marshmallows, crackers, and other human fare from car windows. Having lost their natural fear of people, these unnaturally performing bears became bold in pursuing human food, resulting in frequent visitor injuries, property damage, and sadly, the killing of "problem" bears.

In the early 1970s, the last park garbage dump was closed and prohibition of roadside feeding began. Now, the park's black and grizzly bears are thriving on the plants and animals that Nature provides for them. They have returned to more natural bear behaviors. While a few years ago visitors were virtually certain to see a bear or two on a drive through the park, today there is no guarantee. We must be satisfied and reassured by the simple knowledge that they are here, and pleasantly surprised if one comes our way.

Adult gray wolf, winter.

WOLVES

A deep chesty bawl echoes from rimrock to rimrock, rolls down the mountain, and fades into the far blackness of the night. It is an outburst of wild defiant sorrow, and of contempt for all the adversities of the world…only the mountain has lived long enough to listen objectively to the howl of a wolf.
—Aldo Leopold, *Thinking Like a Mountain*

For far too many years, the mountains and valleys of Yellowstone failed to hear the song of the wolf. The gray wolf was native to Yellowstone National Park at the time of its establishment, but intensive control efforts eliminated it from the park by the 1940s. Like snakes and spiders, the wolf was an animal that few people loved. Over the years, attitudes changed, people became more enlightened, and concerted efforts to return the noble wolf to its niche in the park ecosystem resulted in successful restoration of this grand predator in 1995.

In the past, wolf packs roamed from the Arctic tundra to Mexico, but as people occupied and developed more of the landscape, wolves were regarded as dangerous predators. Loss of habitat and deliberate extermination programs, like those undertaken by the government in Yellowstone, led to their demise. Now, we have a better understanding of the role that the wolf plays in a naturally functioning ecosystem, where predator-prey relationships are essential parts of food chains. The gray wolf is considered an endangered species throughout its historic range in the lower 48 states, except in Minnesota, where large populations thrive.

Yellowstone was ideally suited as a site for wolf restoration. It was large. It had an abundant population of prey animals. And, the wolf had been part of the native fauna. In early 1995 and 1996, 31 gray wolves from Canada were released in Yellowstone—the first to roam Yellowstone since the 1930s. The goal is to maintain at least 10 breeding wolf pairs in the Greater Yellowstone Ecosystem and in each of the two other recovery areas in central Idaho and northwestern Montana.

Yellowstone's restored wolf population has thrived, with relatively few conflicts with human activities adjacent to the park. As of late 1999, about 160 wolves roamed the monitored area, including dozens of pups born the previous spring. The wolves were traveling in at least nine packs, with several solitary wolves wandering alone, seeking mates, or in groups that did not have a breeding pair.

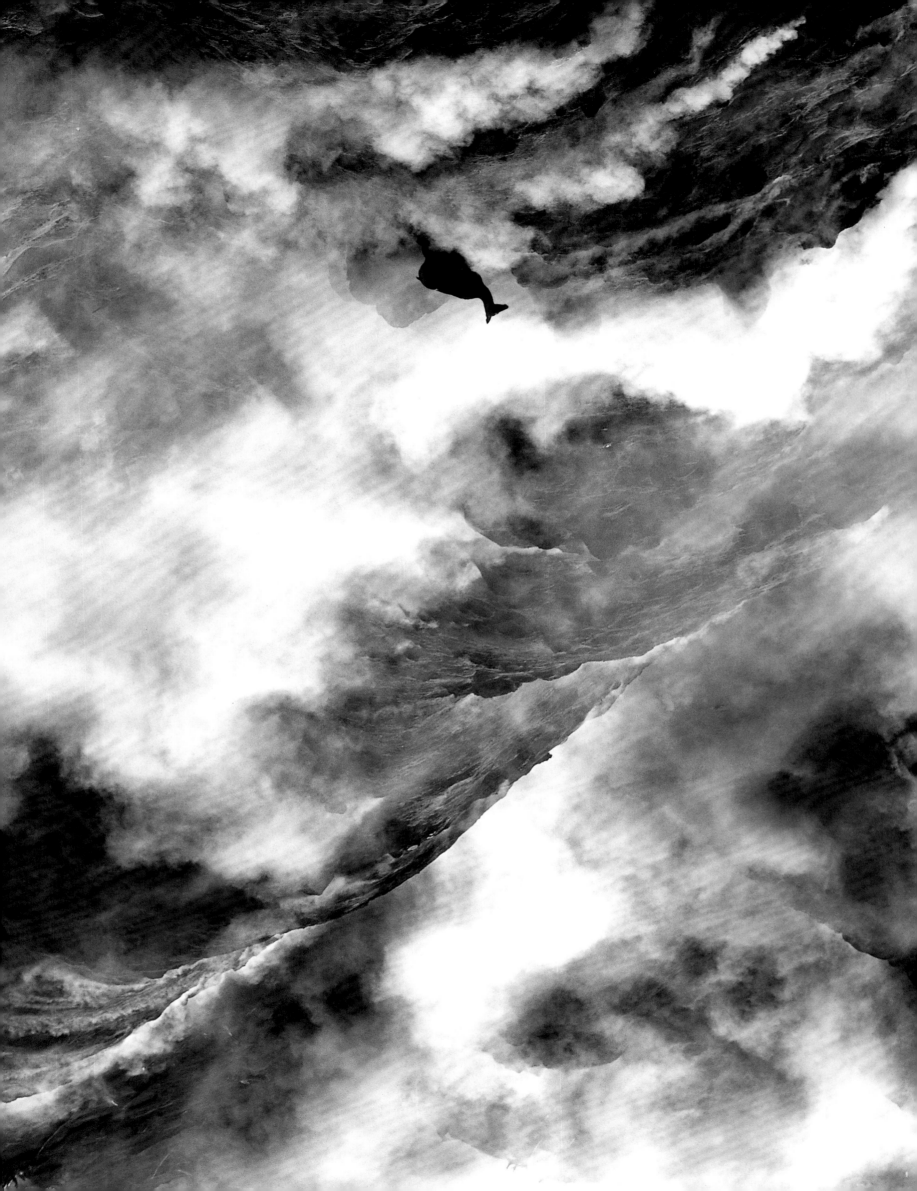

THE WATERS OF YELLOWSTONE:

Sunset at Clepsydra Geyser, Lower Geyser Basin.   PHOTO © GLENN VAN NIMWEGEN

It was then that I felt the cold needles of the alpine springs at my
fingertips, and the warmth of the Gulf pulling me southward…
flowing like the river was flowing, grain by grain, mountain by
mountain, down to the sea. —Loren Eiseley, *The Immense Journey*

I am beyond the park boundary, high on Two-Ocean Plateau, about to drop down into the Thorofare country. Overhead, wisps of water vapor swirl about and build into clouds that darken with their burden of water and eventually release it as rain, some of it falling into the small nameless stream nearby. The stream is an anomaly. For a short distance, it straddles the backbone of the continent, then it splits and becomes two streams dubbed Atlantic Creek and Pacific Creek. Nature is fickle. Depending on currents and subtle changes in the streambed, water flows into one branch or the other, and ultimately to one of the namesake oceans, linking Yellowstone with a much larger world of water.

There are lakes in this country—big ones like Yellowstone, Shoshone, Lewis, and Hart. Yet, they are just temporary waypoints for moving water. It is streams and rivers that best celebrate the power and artistry of water and how it has crafted a spectacular landscape.

As I follow Atlantic Creek, its increasing volume and velocity remind me that gravity is the force and water the instrument. Atlantic Creek will eventually find its way to the stunning Thorofare Valley. There it will add to the gathering flow of the young Yellowstone River, which rises in the Absaroka Mountain Range on the slopes of Yount Peak (the headwaters of the Missouri, Columbia, and Colorado also rise in Yellowstone). Meandering for several miles through the marshy valley floor, the river surrenders itself to the Southeast Arm of Yellowstone Lake. River water will spend much time in the great lake, mingling with the water added by more than 120 other streams. Eventually—perhaps in years—it will leave the lake far to the north in a reborn Yellowstone River.

Tumbling over Le Hardy Rapids, the larger river moves slowly through Hayden Valley, until it abruptly drops over the Upper and Lower Falls into the Grand Canyon of the Yellowstone and flows northeast to Tower Junction. There, freshened by water brought down from high in the Hoodoo Basin by the Lamar River, the Yellowstone tumbles through the Black Canyon. As it leaves the park it is bolstered a final time with runoff collected by the Gardner River. On northwest slopes, the Gallatin River collects water, and drains out of the park, eventually joining the Yellowstone at its confluence with the Madison and Jefferson Rivers. The Yellowstone River is the last major undammed river in the lower 48 states, flowing 671 miles from its source to the Missouri River.

Thinking about the sojourn of the Yellowstone River, I envision the Madison River and know that the course a river follows is set by topography, not by a compass. At Madison Junction, the north-flowing Firehole River joins the south-flowing Gibbon River to form the Madison River. The Madison flows west and then north to where it joins the Missouri River, which then flows east and then south to join the Mississippi.

The Snake River begins on Two Ocean Plateau, and is later joined by Atlantic Creek's sibling, Pacific Creek. It traces 42 miles through the southern part of Yellowstone National Park, and eventually adds Yellowstone water to the Columbia River.

Geologists believe that Yellowstone Lake originally flowed south into the Snake River. In an ironic geologic twist, fluctuations in the size of a body of molten rock beneath the northern shore is gradually tilting the lake so that it may eventually return its outflow to the Snake River. The image and sound of water tumbling over falls in the Grand Canyon of the Yellowstone is so firmly fixed in my mind that I can scarcely imagine a silent, dry riverbed.

Everywhere in Yellowstone I see reminders that the endless peregrinations of water have shaped this landscape, its life, and its features: stones polished smooth by a tumbling stream; steam rising ethereally above a geyser basin; perennial snow packed deep on high, severe slopes; hardened sediments deposited on the floor of an ancient inland sea concealing the fossilized bones of a

---

OPPOSITE: Lower Yellowstone Falls, Grand Canyon of the Yellowstone. PHOTO © LARRY ULRICH

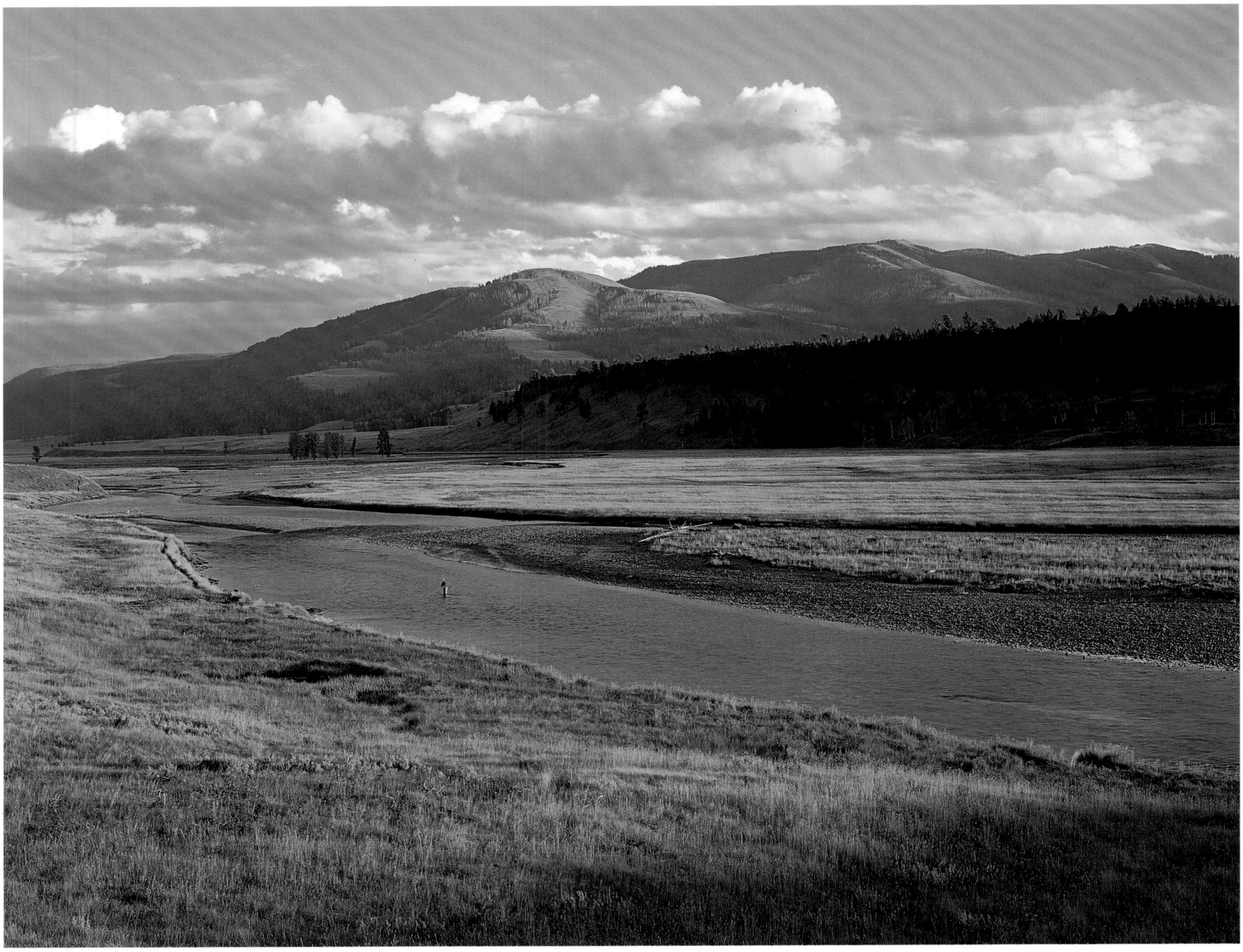

Fly fisherman in the Lamar River, autumn. PHOTO © CARR CLIFTON

prehistoric marine animal. I see small circles spreading outward on the surface of a lake, marking where a trout has risen to a hapless fly. I watch pelicans and cormorants fishing, muskrats and river otters at play. I find chiseled teeth marks on the arrow point stumps of lakeshore trees and examine a well-engineered beaver dam. Each morning I find dew clinging to leaves and blades of grass.

Sometimes water does its work quickly, as in a stream flooding with spring snowmelt. At other times, it moves very slowly. Water trapped in cracks in timberline rocks late in fall freezes and expands during winter, prying off outer layers that fall away onto talus slopes in spring.

Hundreds of small lakes, streams, and cataracts interconnect with their larger counterparts in a network of watery veins that criss-cross and nourish the body of Yellowstone. All of them are part of the perpetual cycle that circulates and exchanges the vital essence among living organisms and the inanimate world.

Steam and runoff from Midway Geyser Basin. PHOTO © JACK DYKINGA

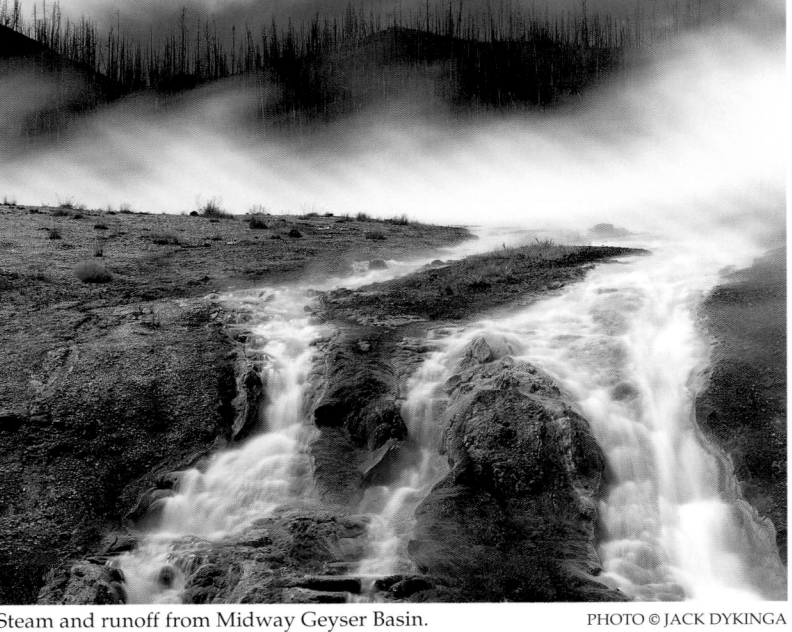

New growth beneath lodgepole forest burnt during the fires of 1988—photo made in 1998.

PHOTO © DIANA STRATTON

THE ROLE OF FIRE

Fire is the reuniting of matter with oxygen. If one bears that in mind, every blaze may be seen as a reunion, an occasion of chemical joy. —Tom Robbins, *Even Cowgirls Get the Blues*

Fire has been a fundamental part of Nature's machinery in Yellowstone since the first tree was scorched by lightning thousands of years ago. Still, until the late summer of 1988, no large fires in recent memory had swept through the largely even-aged, old-growth forest of lodgepole pine. Fire invigorated the system by reducing the old-growth forest, opening the canopy, and releasing nutrients, so that more vibrant pioneer plant species could begin the process of succession again. The fire created community edges, and those edges are biologically rich. Sometimes when I visit Yellowstone I feel like I'm missing something, as if I'm coming into a theater after the movie or play has started. In a way, that is what visitors were doing for decades before the great fires of 1988. Forest succession had been underway for 300 years or so, and the fires were like the curtain rising on the final act of an ecological drama.

Plant and animal populations have inhabited this area since Ice Age glaciers melted 10,000 years ago and have experienced many such natural cyclic events. Yellowstone is an ecosystem adapted to fire and, in some cases, dependent on it. This is particularly true of the extensive forests of lodgepole pine that dominate the Yellowstone landscape.

Lodgepole pines produce two types of cones: one that opens at maturity and a serotinous type that opens only after it has been heated by fire. The serotinous cones ensured a ready seed source for seedling establishment after the 1988 fires.

If fire is excluded long enough, these lodgepole pine forests will be replaced by spruce-fir forests. The large expanses of even-aged lodgepole pine forests in Yellowstone are a good example of how fire affects this Yellowstone forest community.

The first plants to inhabit sites after a fire or other disturbance are called pioneers. The forest canopy must be removed or thinned to allow them to gain a foothold. Other plants growing on the forest floor are adapted to survive at subsistence levels for a long time, but they cannot exist forever under a forest canopy and are dependent on periodic fires to remove the overstory.

Osprey with cutthroat trout in its grasp.

PHOTO © SCOTT McKINLEY

CUTTHROAT & LAKE TROUT

When the first Europeans arrived in Yellowstone, many park waters had no fish populations. During the late 1880s when the U.S. Army administered the newly created Yellowstone National Park, non-native fish were planted in some of the park's lakes, rivers, and streams. At that time lake trout, or Mackinaw, native to the Great Lakes were brought here and planted in Lewis Lake, which had no native fish population.

In the earliest years, Yellowstone Lake had a thriving and healthy population of native cutthroat trout; since then it has supported the premiere cutthroat trout fishery in the nation. Lake trout were never stocked in its waters, yet in 1994 lake trout were discovered in the lake. The lake trout is large, aggressive, and predatory. It could seriously deplete or eliminate the native cutthroat trout population, which might have far-reaching ecological effects on other species. Cutthroat trout are an important food source for more than 40 different species of animals in the ecosystem, including osprey, eagles, pelicans, river otters, and the threatened grizzly bear.

Unlike the cutthroat trout that enters tributary streams to spawn, the lake trout lives in deep water and spawns on the lake bottom, where it is rarely available to the predators that might control it. Biologists believe that a small but growing population of lake trout, and the presence of reproductively mature adults that will add to the population, insures that it will multiply rapidly and potentially overwhelm competitors.

Scientists believe that cutthroat trout comprise 80 percent of a lake trout's diet. They estimate that 50 to 60 cutthroat trout are saved for every lake trout caught. Since lake trout are already established, there is no known way to eliminate them from Yellowstone Lake. Still, biologists believe that the levels of lake trout can be controlled by aggressive gillnetting activities similar to those used by commercial fishermen in the Great Lakes. Perhaps this will maintain the cutthroat trout population at levels sufficient to sustain the wildlife populations that depend on the native species for food. The goal for the lake trout control program is to limit their numbers so that they eat fewer cutthroat trout each year than anglers take home.

OPPOSITE: Tower Falls. PHOTO © J.C. LEACOCK   **PAGE 52 & 53:** Riverside Geyser erupting from the banks of the Firehole River. PHOTO © ROBERT HILDEBRAND

Morning Glory Pool, Upper Geyser Basin.

ALGAE, BACTERIA & SLIME MOLD

Looking down into a caldron of water, or the mouth of a geyser, it is inconceivable that life could survive there. Yet in recent years, scientists have discovered microscopic organisms living in the incredibly hot and inhospitable environments of boiling springs and geyser vents. Some of these one-celled life forms have become the basis of a $500 million industry. It's as if Nature is tired of our preoccupation with her large and spectacular work in Yellowstone and wants to remind us that small things are beautiful and valuable, too. Microbiologists believe the tiny heat-tolerant fauna to be so rich that they refer to microscopic "rain forests" in the sense that we've only just begun to identify the microbes living in hot springs and geysers. They think that we'll discover diversity equal to or greater than that believed to exist in terrestrial rain forests and that these life forms are very similar to the first life forms to have developed on earth.

Visitors accustomed to associating big animals such as bears, elk, and moose with Yellowstone may be surprised to learn that the organisms that have the greatest economic impact on us cannot be seen un-aided. They only become visible when they coalesce into layers of material called bacterial mats, containing biological pigments. The heat-tolerant, or thermophilic, bacteria that live in Yellowstone's hot springs are so small that 500 of them could be placed end to end on the point of a pencil. Microbiologists have learned that the organisms thriving in Yellowstone's thermal features contain enzymes that are stable under extreme temperatures and that they have major implications for medicine and technology. An enzyme from the bacterium *Thermus aquaticus* has been widely used in medical diagnosis and in forensic science (DNA fingerprinting), and several other significant industrial applications are based on enzymes extracted from organisms living in Yellowstone's thermal basins.

Primitive plants are also responsible for the colors in thermal runoff channels and on the edges of hot springs and other features. Single-celled photosynthetic bacteria (cyanobacteria), which thrive at certain temperatures, tell us how hot the water is, with the temperatures generally decreasing outward from the vent. Colors in the hottest waters (180°F. and higher) are usually pale yellow and pinkish-white. At around 160° the shades change to brighter yellows, which blend into oranges at about 145°. Browns and greens begin to show up at temperatures of 120° and lower.

OPPOSITE: Aprons of multi-colored algae around Grand Prismatic Spring, Midway Geyser Basin (aerial view). PHOTO © TOM TILL

WILDFLOWERS

Fireweed. PHOTO © BOB YOUNG

White phlox. PHOTO © GLENN VAN NIMWEGEN

Calypso orchid. PHOTO © ELIZABETH BOEHM

In a land of long winters and deep snow, white is the dominant color during much of the year. But during the brief period when ice and snow relinquish their hold on the landscape to the warming sun, the park is peppered with a kaleidoscopic array of wildflowers.

The fairy-slipper, or Calypso orchid, blooms from May through July. It is typical in cool coniferous forests and bogs of the montane and subalpine forest. Calypso is named for the legendary sea nymph of Homer's *Odyssey*, perhaps because of the secluded sites in which it grows.

While in its vegetative state it is inconspicuous, but when the bitterroot blooms from May through July it is unmistakable. Its scientific name *Lewisia* was given in honor of explorer Meriwether Lewis who collected a specimen in 1806. It was an important food source for American Indians. The bitterroot is the state flower of Montana.

The pinkish blossoms of fireweed—related to the evening primrose—can be seen throughout the park in July and August. It is especially abundant on moist soils in areas disturbed by recent forest fires. A prolific efflorescence of fireweed occurred following the epic fires of 1988. Fireweed was among the first species to appear, even while nearby soil was still smoldering. It provided a colorful contrast to the charred ground and blackened trees.

From April through July, arrowleaf balsamroot, covers many of the park's open slopes with showy, yellow, sunflowerlike blossoms. It is named for the sap in its large, woody root, which has the aroma and texture of balsam fir pitch. American Indians used the root of this plant for treating various diseases, and they ground the seeds into flour to make bread.

From May to June on the Northern Range, the blue blossoms of pasqueflower announce the arrival of spring. The precocious pasqueflower can sometimes be seen pushing up through the snow in late March. The single large purple flower stands atop a stem with leaves near the bottom. Long, silky, straight hairs cover the entire plant.

The Yellowstone sand verbena is of special interest because it is found nowhere else in the world but along the shores of Yellowstone Lake. It grows as a low, matlike covering on sandy soils. Clusters of small white flowers are present from mid-June until late August or early September. Sticky glands cover the plant surfaces causing grains of sand to adhere to them.

Arrowleaf balsamroot. PHOTO © JEFF D. NICHOLAS

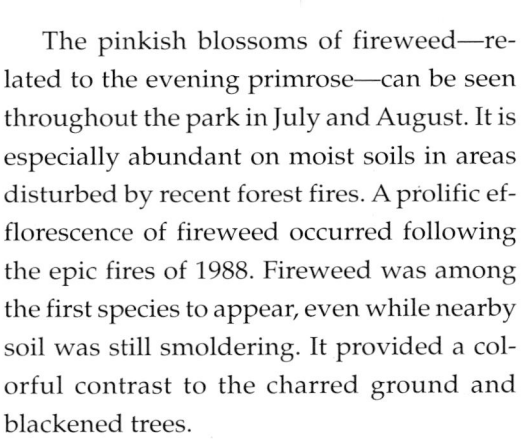

Bitterroot. PHOTO © ELIZABETH BOEHM

Yellow monkeyflower. PHOTO © JEFF GNASS

OPPOSITE: A carpet of heartleaf arnica beneath fire-charred lodgepole pines. PHOTO © JACK DYKINGA

MAMMALS

River otter.   PHOTO © DIANA STRATTON

Bighorn sheep.   PHOTO © JEFF FOOTT

Pronghorns.   PHOTO © DIANA STRATTON

Yellowstone's mammal fauna includes one of two remaining large, self-regulating grizzly bear populations in the lower 48 states. While the population currently hovers at a few hundred individuals, it is perhaps the species most vulnerable to the fragmentation of the ecosystem. The grizzly's smaller relative, the black bear, is present in larger numbers, but neither species is as frequently seen as in the past. This is not necessarily an indication of decreasing numbers. In recent years, more enlightened wildlife management policies have eliminated artificial feeding, a practice that led to the frequent appearance of bears at roadsides and garbage dumps. Deprived of this often unhealthy food source, the bears have simply dispersed back into more remote sections of the park, a much healthier situation for bears and people.

The majestic elk, or wapiti (a Shawnee Indian word) is, without doubt, the most easily and frequently seen large herbivore. The park's elk population varies, but is between 20,000 and 30,000 at its upper optimum level, divided into several migratory herds of varying size. While historic population levels are uncertain, combined with other herds in the region, there may be about 90,000 elk throughout the Greater Yellowstone Ecosystem today—the largest herd in North America.

The largest, free-ranging population of bison remaining in North America (about 2,500 animals) is composed of three herds, which are found in the Lamar Valley, Pelican Valley, and the Hayden and Firehole Valleys. Watching several hundred bison lumber dustily across a valley floor, one can only imagine what the enormous herds that once roamed much of the continent must have looked like. It is estimated that 60 million bison lived on the Great Plains, where they sustained several tribes of Plains Indians. The bison population was reduced to fewer than 50 animals by the beginning of the 20th century. The bison was saved and drawn back from the edge of extinction in the refuge of Yellowstone. The American bison is commonly called the buffalo, a name more correctly applied to the cape buffalo of Africa. Next to the elk, it is the most frequently observed large mammal.

Other hoofed mammals found in smaller populations include mule and white-tailed deer (mainly at lower elevations), bighorn sheep, pronghorn, and Shira's moose. Moose are often encountered in open meadows and along stream courses. They are odd-looking creatures, whose clumsy appearance belies a surprising grace and swiftness of foot. Moose may be seen in Willow Park, south of Mammoth, in meadows near Canyon Village and Lake, and in the Snake River area to the south.

Like its larger elk relatives, the brownish

Pika.   PHOTO © JEFF FOOTT

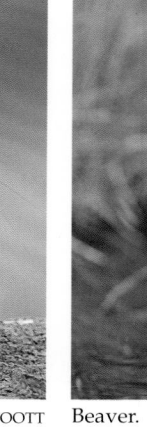

Beaver.   PHOTO © JEFF FOOTT

Bull Shira's moose.   PHOTO © DIANA STRATTON

Porcupines. PHOTO © TOM & PAT LEESON

Badgers. PHOTO © DIANA STRATTON

Uinta ground squirrels. PHOTO © DIANA STRATTON

mule deer (also commonly called the black-tailed deer) summers at higher elevations but moves down to warmer, sheltered valleys during the long winters. Unlike the white-tailed deer (seen in fewer numbers and at lower elevations, and sporting a characteristic large "flag" tail), the mule deer has a short, black tail, and very large ears. Deer tend to move downslope to watercourses at twilight and early evening and can become a traffic hazard.

Sure-footed and acrobatic, the bighorn sheep may be seen negotiating the steep walls of the Gardner River canyon near Mammoth Hot Springs during the winter. In summer, it moves to higher elevations. A summer hike to the summit of Mount Washburn—a rewarding trip on its own merits—may result in a surprise closeup encounter with a group of bighorns.

The pronghorn antelope frequents the lower, drier areas, especially to the north.

Perhaps more than any other Yellowstone ungulate, it looks like it was displaced from the Serengeti. It is distinctively colored tan and white. The pronghorn is incredibly fast—capable of quickly reaching speeds of 60 miles an hour—and can leap nearly 30 feet in a single bound.

A seventh large ungulate was introduced to the region but is seldom seen. The shaggy, white-coated mountain goat is a creature of high elevations, such as the Beartooth Mountains. Although successful in this environment, it is not a part of Yellowstone's native fauna as it is farther to the north in Glacier National Park.

There are more than 50 small mammals living in Yellowstone. In numbers they far exceed their showier, more charismatic, relatives. Many of them are so small and secretive that they are seldom seen. Sometimes their trails, burrows, or nests are the only evidence of their presence. Still, they are key

to the survival of the larger critters. While some, such as bats and pygmy shrews, are voracious predators, many small mammals are eaten by larger predators. Examine the menu of the coyote. Red-backed voles, pocket gophers, snowshoe hares, squirrels, deer mice, shrews, and bats frequently appear as entrees. White bark pine seeds harvested by red squirrels and cached in middens throughout the forest are sought out by hungry grizzly bears emerging from hibernation.

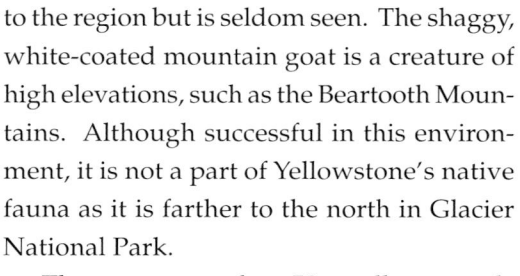

Black bear. PHOTO © JEFF FOOTT

Red fox. PHOTO © TOM & PAT LEESON

Grizzly bear and cub. PHOTO © DIANA STRATTON

PAGE 60 & 61: Bison in grasslands near Lower Geyser Basin. PHOTO © CAROL POLICH

BIRDS

White pelican.   PHOTO © SCOTT McKINLEY

Peregrine falcon.   PHOTO © DIANA STRATTON

Western tanager.   PHOTO © JEFF FOOTT

Since the establishment of Yellowstone in 1872, 311 species of birds have been identified in the park. The population includes a surprising diversity of birds, large and small, colorful and dull, showy and inconspicuous, common and rare. One hundred and forty eight species nest in the park. They include the peregrine falcon, only recently removed from federal endangered species listing, and the still-listed bald eagle. The whooping crane, another endangered species, is found in the park, but it is not known whether it nests in Yellowstone. Other birds of special interest include trumpeter swans, ospreys, common loons, harlequin ducks, great blue herons, great gray owls, and colonial nesting birds.

Captive-bred peregrine falcons were released in Yellowstone from 1983 to 1987, and the number of known nests, or eyries, in the park increased from one in 1984 to 13 in 1998. Peregrine falcons live in Yellowstone from April through October and migrate to Central or South America in winter. In 1999, it was announced that the species had recovered sufficiently to permit removal from the endangered species list.

Bald eagles thrive in the Greater Yellowstone Ecosystem. The number of active nests almost tripled between 1982 and 1998, when 21 of the ecosystem's 91 bald eagle pairs nested in the park.

Early in the 1900s, habitat destruction and commercial hunting led to the near extinction of the trumpeter swan in the lower 48 states. Unfortunately, the Greater Yellowstone population has declined in recent years. The summer nesting population in the park, which numbered 45 swans at times during the 1980s, rarely exceeds 25 now. The winter population, increased by migrant birds from elsewhere in the greater ecosystem, and from Canada, has varied from 60 to several hundred swans.

The Molly Islands in the Southeast Arm of Yellowstone Lake provide an isolated and secure nesting area for colonial birds. Rocky Island and Sandy Island have colonies of American white pelicans, double-breasted cormorants, Caspian terns, and California gulls. Common loons have nested on Peale Island.

More than 100 of the bird species that can be found in Yellowstone during the summer, including the osprey and the peregrine falcon, spend the winter in Mexico and Central America.

One of America's three remaining populations of whooping cranes is in the Greater Yellowstone Ecosystem, but it is at risk. Sadly, at the end of 1998 only four whooping cranes were known to live in the Yellowstone region.

Great blue heron.   PHOTO © DIANA STRATTON

Great gray owl family.   PHOTO © JEFF FOOTT

Trumpeter swan.   PHOTO © SCOTT MCKINLEY

RESOURCES & INFORMATION

EMERGENCY & MEDICAL:
24-HOUR EMERGENCY MEDICAL SERVICE
Dial 911 *(From hotel rooms dial 9-911)* or (307) 344-7381

MAMMOTH CLINIC *(Open year-round)*
(307) 344-7965

ROAD CONDITIONS:
IN THE PARK	(307) 344-7381
IDAHO	(888) 432-7623
WYOMING	(307) 772-0824
MONTANA	(800) 226-7623

FOR MORE INFORMATION:
NATIONAL PARKS ON THE INTERNET:
www.nps.gov

YELLOWSTONE NATIONAL PARK
PO Box 168
Yellowstone National Park, WY 82190-0168
(307) 344-7381, TDD (307) 344-2386
www.nps.gov/yell

YELLOWSTONE ASSOCIATION
PO Box 117
Yellowstone, WY 82190
(307) 344-2296
www.yellowstoneassociation.org

YELLOWSTONE ASSOCIATION INSTITUTE
PO Box 117
Yellowstone National Park, WY 82190
www.yellowstoneassociation.org/yellinst.htm

GREATER YELLOWSTONE COALITION
PO Box 1874
Bozeman, MT 59771
(406) 586-1593
www.greateryellowstone.org

THE YELLOWSTONE PARK FOUNDATION
37 East Main, Suite 4
Bozeman, MT 59715
(406) 586-6303
www.ypf.org

LODGING INSIDE THE PARK:
YELLOWSTONE NATIONAL PARK LODGES
PO Box 165
Yellowstone National Park, WY 82190
(307) 344-7311, TDD (307) 344-5395
www.travelyellowstone.com

CAMPING INSIDE THE PARK:
YELLOWSTONE NATIONAL PARK LODGES
P O Box 165
Yellowstone, WY 82190
(307) 344-7311, TDD (307) 344-5395
www.travelyellowstone.com

CAMPING & OTHER SUPPLIES
HAMILTON STORES, INC.
PO Box 250
West Yellowstone, MT 59758
(406) 646-7325
www.hamiltonstores.com

LODGING OUTSIDE THE PARK:
CODY COUNTRY CHAMBER OF COMMERCE
(307) 587-2777, (307) 527-6228 (FAX)
www.codychamber.org

EASTERN IDAHO VISITOR
INFORMATION CENTER
505 Lindsey Blvd.
Idaho Falls, ID 83402
(208) 523-1010, (800) 634-3246
www.ifcofc@ida.net

GARDINER CHAMBER OF COMMERCE
(406) 848-7971
www.gardinerchamber.com

JACKSON HOLE CHAMBER OF COMMERCE
(307) 733-3316, (307) 733-5585 (FAX)
www.jacksonhole.com

COOKE CITY/SILVER GATE, MONTANA
CHAMBER OF COMMERCE
(406) 838-2495

WEST YELLOWSTONE CHAMBER OF COMMERCE
(406) 646-7701
www.westyellowstonechamber.com

CAMPING OUTSIDE THE PARK:
AMFAC PARKS & RESORTS
PO Box 165
Aurora, CO 80014
(303) 29-PARKS
www.amfac.com

BRIDGER-TETON NATIONAL FOREST
(307) 739-5500
www.fs.fed.us/btnf/

GALLATIN NATIONAL FOREST
(406) 587-6701
www.fs.fed.us/r4

SHOSHONE NATIONAL FOREST
(307) 527-6241, TDD (307) 578-1294
www.fs.fed.us/r4

TARGHEE NATIONAL FOREST
(208) 624-3151
www.fs.fed.us/tnf/

OTHER REGIONAL SITES:
BIGHORN CANYON NAT'L RECREATION AREA
(406) 666-2412
www.nps.gov/bica/

CRATERS OF THE MOON N.M.
(208) 527-3257
www.nps.gov/crmo/home.htm

DEVILS TOWER N.M.
(307) 467-5283
www.nps.gov/deto/

GLACIER NATIONAL PARK
(406) 888-7800, (406) 888.7806
www.nps.gov/glac/

GRAND TETON NATIONAL PARK
(307) 739-3300, TDD (307) 739-3400
www.nps.gov/grte/

LITTLE BIGHORN BATTLEFIELD
NATIONAL MONUMENT
(406) 638-2621
www.nps.gov/libi/

NATIONAL ELK REFUGE
(307) 733-9212

NEZ PERCE NATIONAL HISTORICAL PARK
(208) 843-2261: Spalding, ID
(406) 689-3155: Wisdom, MT
(406) 357-3130: Chinook, MT
www.nps.gov/nepe

SUGGESTED READING:
Anderson, Roger, and Carol Shively Anderson. *A RANGER'S GUIDE TO YELLOWSTONE DAY HIKES.* Helena, MT: Montana Magazine. 2000

Bryan, T. Scott. *GEYSERS: WHAT THEY ARE AND HOW THEY WORK.* Niwot, CO: Roberts Rinehart, Inc. Publishers 1990.

Carr, Mary and Sharon Eversman. *ROADSIDE ECOLOGY OF GREATER YELLOWSTONE* Missoula, MT: Mountain Press Publishing Co. 1991.

Craighead, Frank C., Jr. *FOR EVERYTHING THERE IS A SEASON: THE SEQUENCE OF NATURAL EVENTS IN THE YELLOWSTONE-GRAND TETON AREA.* Helena, MT: Falcon Publishing Co. 1994.

Cundall, Alan W. and Lystrup, Herbert T. *HAMILTON'S GUIDE TO YELLOWSTONE NATIONAL PARK.* West Yellowstone, MT: Hamilton Stores, Inc. 1999.

Fritz, William J. *ROADSIDE GEOLOGY OF THE YELLOWSTONE COUNTRY.(1985).* Missoula, MT: Mountain Press Publishing Co. 1991.

Haines, Aubrey L., ed. *OSBORNE RUSSELL'S JOURNAL OF A TRAPPER.* Lincoln, NE: University of Nebraska Press. 1965.

Hirschmann, Fred. *YELLOWSTONE.* (1982). Reprint. Portland, OR: Graphic Arts Center Publishing. 1990.

McNamee, Thomas. *THE RETURN OF THE WOLF TO YELLOWSTONE.* New York, NY: Henry Holt. 1998.

Pritchard, James A. *PRESERVING YELLOWSTONE'S NATURAL CONDITIONS: SCIENCE AND THE PERCEPTION OF NATURE.* Lincoln, NB: University of Nebraska Press. 1999.

Schullery, Paul. *SEARCHING FOR YELLOWSTONE: ECOLOGY AND WONDER IN THE LAST WILDERNESS.* New York, NY: Houghton, Mifflin. 1999.

Wuerthner, George. *YELLOWSTONE AND THE FIRES OF CHANGE.* Salt Lake City, UT: Haggis House. 1988.

Yellowstone Association. *YELLOWSTONE: THE OFFICIAL GUIDE TO TOURING AMERICA'S FIRST NATIONAL PARK.* Mammoth, WY: Yellowstone Association. 1997.

ACKNOWLEDGMENTS:

Many thanks to National Park Service employees Diane Chalfant (Chief of Interpretation), Linda Young, Susan Kraft, Jon Dahlheim, and Jim Peaco as well as Debbie Thomas of the Yellowstone Association, Eric Robinson, and Lynnette Emborg. As always, a huge thank you to all the photographers who shared their imagery with me during the editing of this publication.   —J.D.N.

PRODUCTION CREDITS:

Author: George B. Robinson
Editor: Nicky Leach
Book Design: Jeff D. Nicholas
Photo Editors: Jeff D. Nicholas and
              Marcia Huskey
Illustrations: Darlece Cleveland
Illustration Graphics: Marcia Huskey
Printing Coordination: Sung In Printing
              America, Inc.

ISBN 1-58071-033-6 (Paper)
ISBN 1-58071-034-4 (Cloth)
COPYRIGHT 2001 BY:
Panorama International Productions, Inc.
4988 Gold Leaf Drive
Mariposa, CA 95338

Sierra Press is an imprint of
Panorama International Productions, Inc.

SIERRA PRESS

4988 Gold Leaf Drive
Mariposa, CA 95338
(209) 966-5071, 966-5073 (Fax)
e-mail: siepress@yosemite.net

VISIT OUR WEBSITE AT:
www.nationalparksusa.com

SIERRA PRESS

OPPOSITE:
Trumpeter swans in flight.
PHOTO © JEFF FOOTT
BACK COVER:
Bison on hillside.
PHOTO © JEFF VANUGA